Microwave Magic

Appetizers and Side Dishes

Grolier Limited
TORONTO

Contributors to this series:

Recipes and Technical Assistance:
École de cuisine Bachand-Bissonnette
Cooking consultants:
Denis Bissonette
Michèle Émond
Dietician:
Christiane Barbeau
Photos:
Laramée Morel Communications
Audio-Visuelles
Design:
Claudette Taillefer
Assistants:
Julie Deslauriers
Philippe O'Connor
Joan Pothier
Accessories:
Andrée Cournoyer
Writing:
Communications La Griffe Inc.
Text Consultants:
Cap et bc inc.
Advisors:
Roger Aubin
Joseph R. De Varennes
Gaston Lavoie
Kenneth H. Pearson

Assembly:
Carole Garon
Vital Lapalme
Jean-Pierre Larose
Carl Simmons
Gus Soriano
Marc Vallières
Production Managers:
Gilles Chamberland
Ernest Homewood
Production Assistants:
Martine Gingras
Catherine Gordon
Kathy Kishimoto
Peter Thomlison
Art Director:
Bernard Lamy
Editors:
Laurielle Ilacqua
Susan Marshall
Margaret Oliver
Robin Rivers
Lois Rock
Jocelyn Smyth
Donna Thomson
Dolores Williams
Development:
Le Groupe Polygone Éditeurs Inc.

We wish to thank the following firms, PIER I IMPORTS and LE CACHE POT, for their contribution to the illustration of this set.

The series editors have taken every care to ensure that the information given is accurate. However, no cookbook can guarantee the user successful results. The editors cannot accept any responsibility for the results obtained by following the recipes and recommendations given.

Canadian Cataloguing in Publication Data

Main entry under title:

Appetizers and side dishes

(Microwave magic ; 15)
Translation of: Entrées et hors-d'œuvre.
Includes index.
ISBN 0-7172-2436-8

1. Cookery (Appetizers).   2. Cookery (Entrées).   3.
Microwave cookery.
I. Series: Microwave magic (Toronto, Ont.) ; 15.

TX832.E6813 1988   641.8'1   C88-094214-2

Contents

Microwave Magic is a multi-volume set, with each volume devoted to a particular type of cooking. So, if you are looking for a chicken recipe, you simply go to one of the two volumes that deal with poultry. Each volume has its own index, and the final volume contains a general index to the complete set.

Microwave Magic puts over twelve hundred recipes at your fingertips. You will find it as useful as the microwave oven itself. Enjoy!

Note from the Editor

How to Use this Book
The books in this set have been designed to make your job as easy as possible. As a result, most of the recipes are set out in a standard way.

We suggest that you begin by consulting the information chart for the recipe you have chosen. You will find there all the information you need to decide if you are able to make it: preparation time, cost per serving, level of difficulty, number of calories per serving and other relevant details. Thus, if you have only 30 minutes in which to prepare the evening meal, you will quickly be able to tell which recipe is possible and suits your schedule.

The list of ingredients is always clearly separated from the main text. When space allows, the ingredients are shown together in a photograph so that you can make sure you have them all without rereading the list—another way of saving your valuable time. In addition, for the more complex recipes we have supplied photographs of the key stages involved either in preparation or serving.

All the dishes in this book have been cooked in a 700 watt microwave oven. If your oven has a different wattage, consult the conversion chart that appears on the following page for cooking times in different types of oven. We would like to emphasize that the cooking times given in the book are a minimum. If a dish does not seem to be cooked enough, you may return it to the oven for a few more minutes. Also, the cooking time can vary according to your ingredients: their water and fat content, thickness, shape and even where they come from. We have therefore left a blank space on each recipe page in which you can note the cooking time that suits you best. This will enable you to add a personal touch to the recipes that we suggest and to reproduce your best results every time.

Although we have put all the technical information together at the front of this book, we have inserted a number of boxed entries called **MICROTIPS** throughout to explain particular techniques. They are brief and simple, and will help you obtain successful results in your cooking.

With the very first recipe you try, you will discover just how simple microwave cooking can be and how often it depends on techniques you already use for cooking with a conventional oven. If cooking is a pleasure for you, as it is for us, it will be all the more so with a microwave oven. Now let's get on with the food.

The Editor

Key to the Symbols
For ease of reference, the following symbols have been used on the recipe information charts.

The pencil symbol ✏ is a reminder to write your cooking time in the space provided.

Level of Difficulty

🍴 Easy

🍴🍴 Moderate

🍴🍴🍴 Complex

Cost per Serving

$ Inexpensive

$ $ Moderate

$ $ $ Expensive

Power Levels

All the recipes in this book have been tested in a 700 watt oven. As there are many microwave ovens on the market with different power levels, and as the names of these levels vary from one manufacturer to another, we have decided to give power levels as a percentage. To adapt the power levels given here, consult the chart opposite and the instruction manual for your oven.

Generally speaking, if you have a 500 watt or 600 watt oven you should increase cooking times by about 30% over those given, depending on the actual length of time required. The shorter the original cooking time, the greater the percentage by which it must be lengthened. The 30% figure is only an average. Consult the chart for detailed information on this topic.

Power Levels

HIGH: 100% - 90%	Vegetables (except boiled potatoes and carrots) Soup Sauce Fruits Browning ground beef Browning dish Popcorn
MEDIUM HIGH: 80% - 70%	Rapid defrosting of precooked dishes Muffins Some cakes Hot dogs
MEDIUM: 60% - 50%	Cooking tender meat Cakes Fish Seafood Eggs Reheating Boiled potatoes and carrots
MEDIUM LOW: 40%	Cooking less tender meat Simmering Melting chocolate
DEFROST: 30% **LOW: 30% - 20%**	Defrosting Simmering Cooking less tender meat
WARM: 10%	Keeping food warm Allowing yeast dough to rise

Cooking Time Conversion Chart

700 watts	600 watts*
5 s	11 s
15 s	20 s
30 s	40 s
45 s	1 min
1 min	1 min 20 s
2 min	2 min 40 s
3 min	4 min
4 min	5 min 20 s
5 min	6 min 40 s
6 min	8 min
7 min	9 min 20 s
8 min	10 min 40 s
9 min	12 min
10 min	13 min 30 s
20 min	26 min 40 s
30 min	40 min
40 min	53 min 40 s
50 min	66 min 40 s
1 h	1 h 20 min

* There is very little difference in cooking times between 500 watt ovens and 600 watt ovens.

Appetizers: Delicate and Delightful

Appetizers, hors d'oeuvres, entrées—what is the precise meaning of these terms? The truth of the matter is that in modern culinary terminology there is a great deal of overlap between them; we shall therefore try to eliminate some of the resulting confusion. Appetizers include any food that is served as a starter, in other words, prior to the main meal, and they are frequently served in individual portions at the table. We tend to think of hors d'oeuvres as finger food, passed around on platters to be shared and eaten without the aid of dishes or cutlery while enjoying a pre-dinner drink and a chat with fellow guests. In spite of this minor distinction between the two, it is obvious that hors d'oeuvres may certainly be considered appetizers as well. The term *entrée* on the other hand, is probably the most confusing of all, and with very good reason. Literally meaning "entrance" it, also, implies a pre-dinner dish, which is the way it is actually used in France and many other European countries. But North American restaurateurs have thoroughly confused the issue by using this term to describe the main courses on their menus.

We have chosen to use the word "appetizer" to describe many of the recipes in the pages that follow, be they sit-down dishes served at the table or bite-size food served prior to the meal in the living room. We have also included some recipes for what we would consider side dishes, too filling to be used as appetizers but appropriate for serving separately, as accompaniments to the main course.

Appetizers may be served hot or cold and, whether offered in individual portions or on platters to be shared, are intended as an introduction to the meal; they should therefore be designed to whet the appetite and not to satisfy it. They can be simple or quite elaborate, setting the tone for a quiet supper or for a large reception. Representing the culinary talents of their creator, appetizers are meant to stimulate.

Appetizers should be chosen to harmonize with the dishes that are to follow. Certain flavors and textures do not blend well and care should be taken to balance the appetizer with the main dish. For example, if a heavily seasoned main dish is to be served, it should not be preceded by an appetizer containing a great deal of garlic; it is obvious that in this case a lighter starter would be more appropriate.

Care should also be taken when alternating hot and cold dishes. A balanced meal, prepared with imagination and flair, will happily combine different flavors and textures.

It has become very much in vogue to serve only small hors d'oeuvres and other appetizers at receptions and parties. In the nouvelle cuisine style of cooking, based on traditional culinary principles adapted to today's tastes, light appetizers are frequently served before a substantial main dish and, in the same vein, hot starters precede a cold meal.

Appetizers, finger food or otherwise, should always be prepared from ingredients of the highest quality. To avoid any disagreeable surprises platters of fresh vegetables should be prepared at the last minute, minimizing their contact with air and the risk of discoloration and loss of flavor. It is therefore important to take every precaution against the harmful effects of Mother Nature, who does not always respect the requirements of good cooking. The golden rule of good cooking is that all the ingredients used be at their peak of freshness. Then, the success of the meal depends on a balance of flavors and textures.

The wines to be served with appetizers should be chosen as carefully as the appetizers themselves. Dry white wines, sparkling wines and kir (white wine with cassis liqueur) complement light starters quite nicely.

Finally, whether hot or cold, appetizers are to a meal what sauces are to a dish—an indispensable delight.

Appetizer Secrets

Whether you prefer Coquilles Saint-Jacques, a tray of cold meats or a vegetable puff pastry, traditional appetizers or more exotic ones, it is helpful to be familiar with the range of ingredients frequently used in preparing them. Their methods of preparation vary from very simple to very complex.

Fresh ingredients, subtle seasonings, creamy sauces, flavorful stuffings, light pastries—these are some of the ingredients that tickle the gourmet's palate. Vegetables (raw or cooked), eggs, fish, seafood, meat and poultry topped with smooth sauces, served with mayonnaise or sprinkled with butter and lemon juice are all delicious introductions to a meal.

Many vegetables and hard-boiled eggs can be hollowed out and filled to make attractive baskets for appetizers in place of the small ramekins usually used. Meats, chopped vegetables, nuts, breadcrumbs and spices all make delicious stuffings. A good stuffing is always appreciated and is also a clever way of combining a variety of ingredients, not to mention using up leftovers. Dry bread, toasted and crumbled, and cooked rice or vegetables originally used to make soups can all be re-used in stuffings.

Stuffings should be always firm enough to form small balls without falling apart; the use of some fat or a creamy ingredient will hold the dry ingredients together. Beaten eggs, cream cheese and butter can be added to the dry ingredients to bind the filling. Eggs can be added to rice or seafood and will not alter their flavor. To bind stuffings made with ground meat and puréed vegetables use small quantities of breadcrumbs or flour. Crushed nuts are ideal for stuffings made with cream cheese and finely chopped vegetables. Garlic and parsley are important ingredients in most stuffings; other seasonings used vary with the type of stuffing prepared.

Sauces are an important element in the preparation of many appetizers. Recipes for sauces are as diverse as their colors, textures and tastes. Stocks thickened with roux (a blend of cooked butter and flour) are the bases for many hot sauces. A béchamel can be prepared with many different variations and may be served with seafood, vegetables or poultry.

Vegetables may be served cooked or uncooked. A purée of carrots or spinach adds color to a sauce or stuffing. Hot or cold, artichokes, zucchini and tomatoes can be served with a filling or used as ingredients. They are irresistible with or without a stuffing.

Seafood also features prominently among appetizers. It may be served cold, in a mousse, in aspic or with a vinaigrette, or it may be served hot, in the shell. Gourmets will enjoy seafood in a sauce or *au gratin*. Lobster or crab shells make attractive containers in which to present appetizers. Fish, crustaceans and mollusks can also be served hot or cold, with piquant sauces, such as those with garlic or tomato, or with more delicate ones, such as white sauces or lemon butter.

The offal from meat or poultry can be set aside and used in terrines or pâtés. Flavorful liver, kidney and sweetbreads can also be served individually on wooden skewers or in a smooth vegetable sauce. Adding lean meat and poultry to such a sauce will serve to enrich it.

Eggs are indispensable in the preparation of appetizers. As well as adding an extremely decorative touch, they can be served hard-boiled or used in fillings and sauces. And of course without eggs there would be no soufflés, crêpes or quiches.

It is also obvious that we must not forget pastry. Tarts and puff pastry cases are very festive indeed and provide us with such delicious appetizers as Crab Vol-au-Vent (page 32).

Cold appetizers range from complicated cooked dishes to simple crudités, refreshing, light starters which can be enjoyed all year round. Raw or cooked vegetables, red or white meat, seafood or fish can all be served cold. In the preparation of cold appetizers eggs, grains and offal are often used, and the best cold stuffings combine fresh, nutritious ingredients. Both the host and guests will enjoy these simple foods. Some vegetables, such as artichokes, potatoes, asparagus and zucchini, should be blanched before being served cold or used as ingredients. Mushrooms and eggplant should be marinated in oil and spices. Avocados are best served raw, cubed or puréed, with a mayonnaise-based dressing and garnished with chopped nuts or seafood.

Pâtés are served, for the most part, on bread or cracker bases as canapés. Aspics, mousses and sauces add distinction to cold appetizers. Aspics are prepared with colorless gelatin set in bouillon or stock. Vegetables, eggs or seafood should be added to the mixture while it is lukewarm and before it is completely set. Suspended in the jelly or carefully arranged in even layers, these food elements form attractive decorative patterns such as flower clusters or geometric checkerboards—whetting the imagination as well as the palate. Mousses are also made with a blend of bouillon and gelatin but the other ingredients are puréed before being added and chilled.

And now, because appetizers are really all about imagination, we present a riddle for you to solve so as to disclose a favorite accompaniment for them. It is made with three main ingredients: the first is a food basic to all cooking that comes in a white shell; the second is a citrus fruit, often used as a garnish for drinks or main dishes; and the third is a golden liquid, a vegetable extract. Combined, these ingredients create a white sauce absolutely indispensable to cold dishes. The answer?

You're right; it's mayonnaise. It can be bought ready made, but homemade mayonnaise will always surpass the store-bought variety in both flavor and consistency.

Vinaigrette is another reputable dressing that is extremely popular. Both mayonnaise and vinaigrette are served over or as an acompaniment to salads, cold fish, raw vegetables and numerous other dishes. In the next few pages you will find recipes for both of these delicious dressings. It should be remembered that sauces are important, even for cold dishes.

There is no limit to the possible combinations and ways of presenting appetizers, whether hot or cold. But one golden rule must always be followed—appetizers should be light and should always complement the dishes to follow. Your own flair and imagination are your best guides in this respect.

Preparing Hot Appetizers

Certain basic combinations of ingredients and methods of preparation are common to all hot appetizers. Stuffings, sauces and pastry shells are integral parts of many. That it would be inappropriate to stuff a pepper with ground meat only is certainly obvious. Breadcrumbs or cooked rice are needed to give some body to the stuffing, such starchy foods providing the necessary texture nad firmness, and other ingredients and seasonings are needed for flavor. Rice, incidentally, can also be used as a main ingredient in appetizers; rice cakes with white sauce and vegetables or a creamy chicken sauce are always delicious.

Vegetable purées blend well with stuffings and sauces. If the vegetables used do not contain starch, however, add rice or potatoes to bind the mixture. When preparing hot appetizers, the vegetables should be boiled before being puréed. Vegetables containing a large amount of water (zucchini or spinach, for example) should be placed in a sieve after they are cooked and all excess water drained so that the stuffing or garnish in which they are to be used doesn't become soggy. Herbs and seasonings add flavor to these purées, which are also enriched by adding melted butter or cream.

Many sauces for appetizers are prepared with the same ingredients that are used in sauces for main dishes. Tomatoes are always popular and tomato sauce is a sure favorite—for pasta, meat loaf or seafood. And, indeed, tomatoes themselves are used in many different ways in the preparation of appetizers. Puréed or cubed, they easily absorb the flavors of such spices as basil, oregano, tarragon and bay leaves, and they take well to smooth substances, such as cream and milk. Olive oil and garlic also mix favorably with this red fruit, which is often mistaken for a vegetable.

To complete this section on preparing hot appetizers the role of pastry, hidden under the sauces and containing delicate fillings or other delicious surprises, must not be excluded. Short pastry and puff pastry are both indispensable to the creation of appetizers. Short pastry is easier to make and is used for tarts and quiches. To make short pastry, combine chunks of butter (not too soft and not too hard) with a mixture of flour and salt in a large bowl. Use two knives to blend the pastry until granular, add the required amount of cold water and mix lightly. Knead the dough gently with your hands and refrigerate for about one hour before rolling out.

Puff pastry, a short pastry that is folded and rolled several times and brushed with butter, is used to make pastry shells. Puff pastry, very light in itself, is suitable for light, more delicate appetizers; if cooked with a filling that is too heavy or too fatty, the pastry would be flat and soggy.

Stuffings

Stuffings can be prepared by combining many different ingredients (nuts, chopped vegetables, seafoods, meat, cheese, eggs and so on) with different aromatic seasonings. They may be served as fillings in vegetables that have been hollowed out, such as zucchini, in the shells of crustaceans or in puff pastry shells.

Short Pastry

Short pastry dough is easy to cook in a microwave oven. Prick the dough in the bottom of the plate with a fork in several places and use a transparent dish so that you can easily check the degree of doneness. The dough is ready when the bottom is dry and opaque.

Carefully place the sheet of dough in a transparent glass pie plate and cut around the edge with a knife.

Although not absolutely essential, brushing the dough with a beaten egg yolk helps prevent the pastry from becoming soggy when it is filled.

Prick the dough in the bottom of the pie plate in several places with a fork before cooking. The dough is ready when the bottom is dry and opaque.

Cold Sauces
for Cold Appetizers

Hors d'oeuvres and canapés are terms frequently used to describe small cold appetizers. They are usually prepared in small individual portions and served with an aperitif. It is absolutely essential that the ingredients used in their preparation be very fresh. Neither the cook nor the guests would be satisfied with limp crudités, tired fish or stale nuts with a bitter taste. So always choose ingredients of the highest quality.

Mayonnaise and vinaigrette are the sauces most often used to accompany salads, seafood and raw vegetables. They also constitute the bases for numerous other sauces; we therefore thought it would be useful to describe the method used to prepare these two basic sauces.

Mayonnaise

There is nothing better than a good homemade mayonnaise and, contrary to common belief, it is really very easy to prepare.

First, separate the eggs, putting the yolks in a large bowl and setting the whites aside for later use. Using a wire whisk, beat the yolks vigorously with a little salt until smooth and thick. Add a little lemon juice, beating continuously. The last stage is the most delicate; add the oil very slowly, drop by drop at first and then in a steady thin stream, continuing to beat vigorously with the whisk. Note that an electric beater may also be used. The mayonnaise is ready when the emulsion is thick and creamy. A little Dijon mustard and white pepper may be added for flavor. (Two egg yolks, 1-1/2 cups of oil and 3 tablespoons of lemon juice will produce 1-1/2 cups of mayonnaise.)

Vinaigrette

The classic vinaigrette is a mixture of oil, vinegar, salt and pepper. But this recipe leaves a great deal of room for imagination. You can add herbs, garlic, onions, capers, anchovies, chopped hard-boiled eggs, mustard (dry or creamy) and so on. Lemon juice may be used instead of vinegar and you can experiment with different kinds of salad oil as well as with different flavors of vinegar. Vinaigrette is served with a number of cold dishes, be they vegetable, meat or fish dishes.

Salt does not dissolve in oil and should therefore be added to the vinegar or lemon juice before the oil is whisked in. Some cooks use coarse salt, which they grind into the salad bowl before adding any oil or vinegar. Use approximately 1 part vinegar or lemon juice to 2 to 3 parts oil.

The flavor, color and consistency of different vinaigrettes will obviously vary with the type of oil and vinegar used in each. Olive oil, sunflower oil, soya oil and corn oil all have very different flavors. Flavored white vinegars, with tarragon for example, or colored vinegars such as wine or cider vinegar, offer a wide range of flavors for different vinaigrettes. Strong mustard, such as Dijon, and chopped hard-boiled eggs can also be added. And of course the variety of spices available to season the vinaigrette is almost limitless. The choice is yours—vary your ingredients and discover the combinations that give your vinaigrette a quality of distinction.

Some Variations on Basic Cold Sauces

Variations

A number of different cold sauces are based on variations of mayonnaise and vinaigrette. Aioli is a mayonnaise laced with garlic, tartar sauce is basic mayonnaise with the addition of chopped olives and pickles and lemon juice, and andalouse is made with mayonnaise, tomato purée and pimento. The French vinaigrette is made with Dijon mustard, the English vinaigrette uses dry mustard, and Roquefort sauce, as its name suggests, is a combination of French vinaigrette and Roquefort cheese.

Preparing Mayonnaise

Separate the eggs, putting the yolks into a large bowl with a little salt. Use a whisk to beat the yolks for several minutes until smooth and somewhat thickened.

Add a little lemon juice and whisk vigorously for 1 to 2 minutes.

Pour the oil in slowly, drop by drop at first, and then in a steady thin steam, beating continuously. The mayonnaise is ready when it is thick and creamy.

Preparing Vinaigrette

In a large bowl, dissolve a little salt in the vinegar or lemon juice.

Add the oil, beating vigorously with a wire whisk.

Add the desired flavoring agents. Garlic, onion, mustard and spices or herbs such as basil, tarragon, thyme, bay leaf, parsley and so on may be used.

Surprisingly Simple Microwave Sauces

Hot sauces are always a delight but are sometimes thought to be difficult to prepare to perfection. Hot sauces do in fact require that certain rules be observed; for example, it is necessary to stir them continuously during the cooking and to carefully control the temperature of the elements on a conventional stove. But microwave cooking eliminates many of the complications inherent in the preparation of hot sauces. It is no longer necessary to stir the sauce constantly during the cooking time; it is, however, important to open the oven door a few times to check the consistency and stir the sauce if required. Cooking times will vary, depending on the amount of liquid used in the recipe.

Since the effect of microwaves on food is more intense than that of electric elements, liquids evaporate less quickly in microwave cooking. For this reason, less liquid is used when preparing sauces that are to be cooked in a microwave oven. It is still very important, however, to respect to the minute the cooking times indicated for each recipe.

In recipes for sauces using roux as a base, the amount of butter, flour and liquid will vary according to the consistency desired (light, medium or thick). Sauces based on roux are prepared in three quick and simple steps, as illustrated on page 17, opposite. To prepare a basic white sauce, first heat the butter in an uncovered dish. Then stir in the flour, blending it well with the butter. Add the milk or other appropriate liquid (white stock or bouillon, wine, vegetable juice, depending on the type of sauce) and beat vigorously. This method produces a smooth sauce, but you must make sure to whisk the sauce several times during the cooking. Béchamel sauce is made from a white roux to which milk and spices (cloves, nutmeg, salt, pepper and bay leaves) are added. Velouté sauce is also a classic white sauce; veal, poultry or fish stock is added to the white roux to make an extremely delicate sauce.

Sauces based on blond or brown roux (butter and flour browned to the desired color) require a longer cooking time for the roux. The butter and flour are combined in the same way as white roux but are cooked for a minute or two, until the desired color is obtained. The liquid, in this case brown stock or broth, is then added in the same way as that for white sauces. The cooking times may vary, depending on the type of sauce being prepared.

Egg-based sauces are also surprisingly simple to prepare. The beaten egg yolks are added to the sauce after it has been cooked in the microwave oven. To obtain a smooth consistency, the egg yolks are beaten with the sauce before it is put back in the microwave oven for a few seconds to heat through (it should not be allowed to boil). Egg-based sauces are known for being especially smooth and rich, their texture is like velvet.

Many hot sauces may be prepared ahead of time and kept in the refrigerator, a practical way of saving time and energy. Exellent when reheated, these sauces are an easy way to dress up an everyday meal. The success of other sauces, that is, those not requiring any thickening agent, such as tomato sauce, depends upon the use of the very freshest ingredients. Check the texture and consistency of the ingredients to be used before deciding on your cooking time, and add them gradually to avoid overcooking.

White Sauce Thickened with Roux

Put the butter (or other fat) into a dish and heat uncovered until melted. The butter should be very hot so that the flour, when added, will cook to some extent.

Remove from the oven and add the flour, mixing well.

Add the liquid (white stock or milk) and whisk to blend the mixture well; return to the oven. Open the oven door at least twice during the cooking time and whisk vigorously to prevent the formation of lumps.

White Sauce Thickened with Egg Yolks

Separate the egg yolks from the whites and beat the yolks until they are smooth.

Remove the cooked white sauce from the oven or, if the sauce was previously cooked and cooled, reheat the desired quantity.

Add the egg yolks to the white sauce, whisking continuously, and put back in the oven. Heat through, whisking several times, but do not allow the sauce to boil or it will curdle.

The Art of Thickening Sauces

There are many ingredients that serve as thickening agents and many methods of thickening a sauce. Roux, a blend of heated butter and flour, is one of the most common thickening agents. A stock (a bouillon obtained by lengthy simmering of fish or meat, vegetables and herbs in water) blended with roux will produce a thick sauce. Creamy sauces such as béchamel are prepared in the same way, with milk or cream replacing the stock. The sauce, regardless of its ingredients, must be whisked several times during the cooking to prevent lumps from forming. As mentioned in the preceding section on sauces, a white roux is obtained by combining melted butter and flour and a blond or brown roux, by cooking the butter and flour for a couple of minutes, until the desired color is obtained.

Kneaded butter, also known as *beurre manié,* is prepared with the same ingredients as roux except they are not cooked. Equal quantities of room temperature butter and flour are kneaded together, usually by hand. This mixture is added to a hot sauce or boiling stock, a very small portion at a time, and beaten vigorously to obtain a smooth emulsion. Flour, cornstarch and arrowroot (a tasteless vegetable derivative) are other starchy products that can be used, dissolved in cold water, to thicken sauces effectively as they cook.

Sauces can also be thickened with a mixture of egg yolks and cream, a thickening agent known as the *liaison.* We suggest that it be diluted with a small amount of the hot sauce before being added to the entire quantity. It is also important to cook the sauce just below the boiling point to prevent it from curdling.

For cooks who prefer light sauces, without flour or fatty ingredients, a vegetable purée works well as a thickening agent. As well as adding flavor and substance to sauces, vegetable purées add substantial color. Purée the cooked vegetables in the blender or food processor before adding them to an herbed stock or sauce. Tomatoes, spinach and carrots, cooked and puréed, are examples of vegetables that blend very nicely with certain sauces.

Hot Appetizers: Simple and Elegant

Hot appetizers are surprisingly fast and simple to prepare in the microwave oven. Whether served before a cold meal or a hot one, appetizers are an important part of every menu, from the simplest to the most refined.

In this volume we have selected a number of appetizer recipes which are sure to go well with your favorite dishes. Seafood and fish lovers will be happy to discover Shrimps au Gratin (page 22), a subtle mixture of shrimps, spinach, wine and cheese, and Scallops in Tomato Sauce (page 24), with a creamy tomato sauce. Mussels Bordelaise (page 26), Coquilles Saint-Jacques (page 28) and our Sardine Appetizer (page 30), prepared with white wine, will all invite instant admiration. Other seafood recipes include crab, frogs' legs and lobster as ingredients. We offer three recipes combining these delicate meats with other savory ingredients. The Crab Vol-au-Vent offered on page 32 comes with an exquisite sauce and the recipe for Frogs' Legs with Wine and Cream (page 34) requires no elaborate preparation. The Eggplant Ragout with Lobster Tails (page 36) is a delicate one, with a very original combination of ingredients.

Stuffings are also celebrated in a variety of our dishes. The Zucchini Stuffed with Veal (page 38) and the Stuffed Vine Leaves (page 42) are prepared with different types of spices and choice ingredients.

Vegetables are also featured in our menus. The recipe for Asparagus (page 54) is accompanied by a choice of mornay sauce, made from a béchamel base and prepared quickly in the microwave, or a béarnaise sauce, both delicious. If you enjoy continental cooking, the recipe for Carrots Basque (page 56) describes an interesting and original way of preparing this vitamin-rich vegetable.

Potatoes can be prepared with many different fillings to make great side dishes. Try them all!

The suggestions you will find in this volume are all designed for microwave cooking. The recipes can be modified to suit your imagination, as long as you follow the basic cooking principles set out in each one. Let your own experience be your guide to success in your cooking!

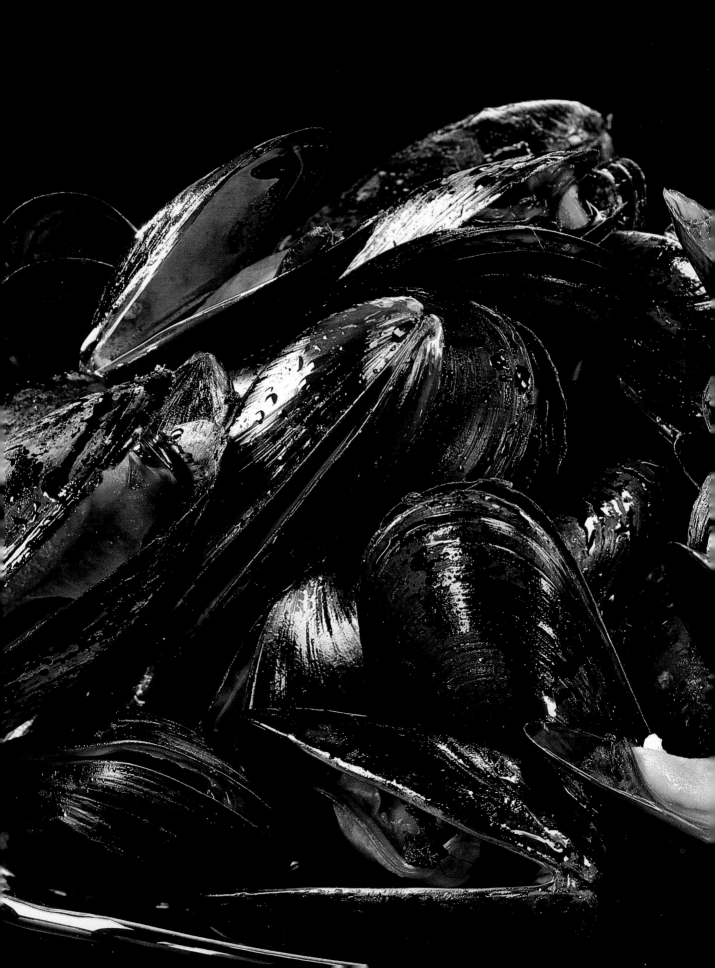

Shrimps au Gratin

Level of Difficulty	🍴
Preparation Time	15 min
Cost per Serving	$ $
Number of Servings	4
Nutritional Value	290 calories 20 g protein 16.5 g lipids
Food Exchanges	3 oz meat 1 vegetable exchange 1 fat exchange
Cooking Time	13 min
Standing Time	None
Power Level	100%
Write Your Cooking Time Here	

MICROTIPS

To Grate Cheese More Easily

Dishes prepared with grated cheese toppings are always popular. You probably have several favorite recipes for *au gratin* dishes that your guests enjoy. However, grating large amounts of cheese is not always a pleasant task. It is much easier if the cheese to be grated is refrigerated before grating; it will then be firmer and is less likely to clog the holes in the grater.

Ingredients

225 g (8 oz) shrimps, shelled and cooked
75 mL (5 tablespoons) butter
225 g (8 oz) spinach
2 green onions, chopped
salt and pepper to taste
45 mL (3 tablespoons) flour
175 mL (3/4 cup) milk
1 clove garlic, crushed
50 mL (1/4 cup) white wine
50 mL (1/4 cup) cheddar cheese, grated
paprika to garnish

Method

— Put 30 mL (2 tablespoons) of the butter in a dish and add the spinach and green onions; cover and cook at 100% for 3 to 5 minutes.
— Drain the cooked vegetables in a sieve and season to taste.
— Place an equal amount of the cooked vegetables into each of four scallop shells and set aside.
— In a bowl, melt the remaining 45 mL (3 tablespoons) of butter at 100% for 30 seconds.
— Add the flour and stir to mix well.
— Stir in the milk, garlic and wine and beat vigorously with a whisk.
— Cook at 100% for 3 to 4 minutes, beating twice with a whisk during the cooking time.
— Add the cooked shrimps to the sauce and stir gently.
— Arrange the mixture in the four shells and sprinkle with the cheddar and paprika.
— Heat the shells at 100% for 2 to 4 minutes, until the cheese is completely melted.

Scallops in Tomato Sauce

Level of Difficulty	⑂⑂
Preparation Time	10 min
Cost per Serving	$ $ $
Number of Servings	6
Nutritional Value	152 calories 15.7 g protein 7 g lipids
Food Exchanges	2 oz meat 1-1/2 fat exchanges
Cooking Time	23 min
Standing Time	None
Power Level	100%, 70%
Write Your Cooking Time Here	

MICROTIPS

For a Creamy Sauce

Cooking sauces in the microwave oven is quite simple but certain techniques will assure a smooth, creamy consistency. Mixtures of cream and tomatoes, such as the sauce served with the scallops in the recipe below, must be stirred during the cooking time to prevent the heavier ingredients from remaining at the bottom of the dish and the lighter ones from rising to the surface.

Ingredients
24 scallops
250 mL (1 cup) tomatoes, peeled and crushed
5 mL (1 teaspoon) parsley, chopped
2 green onions, chopped
1 clove garlic, chopped
5 mL (1 teaspoon) chives, chopped
30 mL (2 tablespoons) butter
125 mL (1/2 cup) 18% cream
salt and pepper to taste

Method
— Drain the tomatoes and set the liquid aside for another use.
— In a small casserole, combine the tomatoes, parsley, green onions, garlic and chives.
— Mix well and cook at 100% for 8 to 10 minutes, breaking the tomatoes up with a fork halfway through the cooking time.
— Add the butter and set aside.
— Pour the cream into a dish and add the scallops; reduce the power to 70% and cook for 7 to 10 minutes, stirring halfway through the cooking time.
— Remove the scallops and arrange on a serving platter.
— Combine the tomato mixture with the cream in which the scallops were cooked; season and heat through at 100% for 2 to 3 minutes, stirring once.
— Pour the hot sauce over the scallops and garnish as desired.

Mussels Bordelaise

Level of Difficulty	(icon)
Preparation Time	15 min
Cost per Serving	$ $
Number of Servings	4
Nutritional Value	116 calories 14 g protein 15 g lipids
Food Exchanges	2 oz meat 3 fat exchanges
Cooking Time	11 min
Standing Time	None
Power Level	100%
Write Your Cooking Time Here	(icon)

MICROTIPS

Cooking Mussels

You can usually identify mussels that are not alive when you are cleaning them. However, if you miss some at this stage you can always check again after they have been cooked. The shells of live mussels will open with heat; discard any mussels the shells of which remain closed after cooking.

Ingredients
675 g (1-1/2 lb) mussels
75 mL (1/3 cup) water
1 small onion, finely chopped
1 tomato, peeled and chopped
50 mL (1/4 cup) butter
125 mL (1/2 cup) white wine
15 mL (1 tablespoon) parsley, chopped
1 bay leaf
2 mL (1/2 teaspoon) cayenne pepper
salt to taste

Method
— Put the mussels into a dish and pour in the water.
— Cover and cook at 100% for 4 to 5 minutes, until the shells open.
— Remove the mussels from the dish and drain them.
— Open the mussels and separate the shells, reserving only the shell to which the mussel is attached.
— Combine all the other ingredients in a casserole and mix well.
— Cook uncovered at 100% for 4 to 6 minutes, breaking up the tomatoes with a fork halfway through the cooking time.
— Pour the sauce over the mussels in their shells and serve immediately.

Coquilles Saint-Jacques

Level of Difficulty	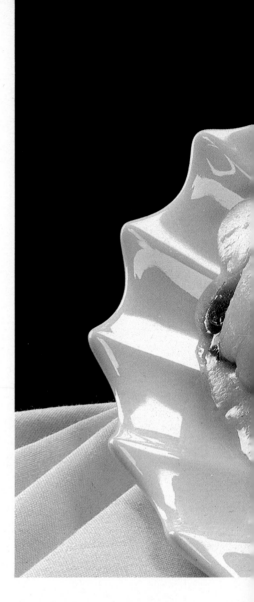 (fork/knife/spoon icons)
Preparation Time	10 min
Cost per Serving	$ $
Number of Servings	8
Nutritional Value	168 calories 16 g protein 7.5 g lipids
Food Exchanges	1.5 oz meat
Cooking Time	14 min
Standing Time	2 min
Power Level	70%, 100%
Write Your Cooking Time Here	

Ingredients
450 g (1 lb) scallops
50 mL (1/4 cup) dry white wine
15 mL (1 tablespoon) green onions, chopped
30 mL (2 tablespoons) butter
30 mL (2 tablespoons) flour
175 mL (3/4 cup) milk or light cream
white pepper to taste
125 mL (1/2 cup) mushrooms, sliced
75 mL (1/3 cup) Gruyère cheese, grated
50 mL (1/4 cup) breadcrumbs
parsley, chopped

Method
— Put the scallops in a dish and sprinkle with the wine; cover and cook at 70% for 5 to 6 minutes, stirring once after 3 minutes.
— Drain the scallops, reserving 50 mL (1/4 cup) of the cooking liquid, and set aside.
— In another dish, cook the green onions in the butter at 100% for 1 minute; add the flour and mix well.
— Add the milk or cream, pepper and cooking liquid, reduce the power level to 70% and cook for 3 to 4 minutes, stirring twice during the cooking time.
— Add the cooked scallops, the mushrooms and the cheese and mix well.
— Pour the mixture into eight scallop shells and sprinkle with the breadcrumbs and parsley.
— Cook at 70% for 2 to 3 minutes, until the contents of the shells are hot.
— Let stand for 2 minutes before serving.

Stir the scallops after 3 minutes of cooking so that they cook evenly.

Drain the cooked scallops, reserving 50 mL (1/4 cup) of the cooking liquid for later use.

MICROTIPS

Another Way to Use Fresh Parsley

Fresh parsley is often sold in quantities that are larger than you need for a single recipe. Leftover parsley may be dried, but why not make a small bouquet and use it as a centerpiece? Place the bouquet in a small pot of water and cover the pot with a napkin to match those on the table and you have a delightful table decoration.

Sardine Appetizer

Level of Difficulty	![difficulty icon]
Preparation Time	5 min
Cost per Serving	$
Number of Servings	2
Nutritional Value	130 calories 13 g protein
Food Exchanges	1.5 oz meat 1 vegetable exchange
Cooking Time	8 min
Standing Time	None
Power Level	70%, 100%
Write Your Cooking Time Here	

Ingredients
115 g (4 oz) sardines
1 carrot, grated
1 onion, finely sliced
2 cloves
125 mL (1/2 cup) white wine
50 mL (1/4 cup) vinegar
1 bouquet garni

Method
— In a dish, combine all the ingredients except the sardines and mix well.
— Cook at 70% for 3 to 4 minutes, until the mixture reaches the boiling point.
— Add the sardines, increase the power to 100% and cook for 3 to 4 minutes.
— Remove the sardines from the vegetable, wine and vinegar mixture.
— Arrange the mixture on a serving platter, place the sardines on top and serve hot or cold, as desired.

These are the ingredients you will need to accompany the sardines in this easy-to-prepare and extremely tasty recipe.

*To serve this dish, remove the
sardines from the vegetable,
wine and vinegar mixture, put
the mixture on a serving platter
and arrange the sardines on top.*

MICROTIPS

How To Stuff a Whole
Fish

Bone and clean the fish
carefully and dry it with
paper towel. Make a
deep incision along the
bottom of the fish
lengthwise, from head to
tail. Spread the fish open
and sprinkle the surface
with lemon juice. Fill the
cavity with the stuffing
you have prepared. With
strong white string, tie
the fish so that it keeps
its shape and the stuffing
stays in place.

Crab Vol-au-Vent

Level of Difficulty	🍴
Preparation Time	10 min
Cost per Serving	$ $
Number of Servings	4
Nutritional Value	368 calories 7.6 g protein 12.7 g lipids
Food Exchanges	0.5 oz meat 2 bread exchanges 3 fat exchanges
Cooking Time	6 min
Standing Time	None
Power Level	100%
Write Your Cooking Time Here	

Ingredients
125 mL (1/2 cup) crabmeat, cooked
30 mL (2 tablespoons) butter
30 mL (2 tablespoons) flour
125 mL (1/2 cup) chicken broth
125 mL (1/2 cup) 10% cream
125 mL (1/2 cup) mushrooms, sliced
15 mL (1 tablespoon) parsley, chopped
15 mL (1 tablespoon) red pimento, chopped
salt and pepper to taste
4 pastry shells, cooked

Method
— In a dish, melt the butter at 100% for 30 seconds, add the flour and mix well.
— Pour in the broth and the cream and beat well with a wire whisk.
— Cook at 100% for 3 to 4 minutes, beating twice with the whisk.
— Add the crabmeat, mushrooms, parsley and red pimento and season to taste. Reheat at 100% for 1 to 2 minutes.
— Pour the mixture into the pastry shells and serve immediately.

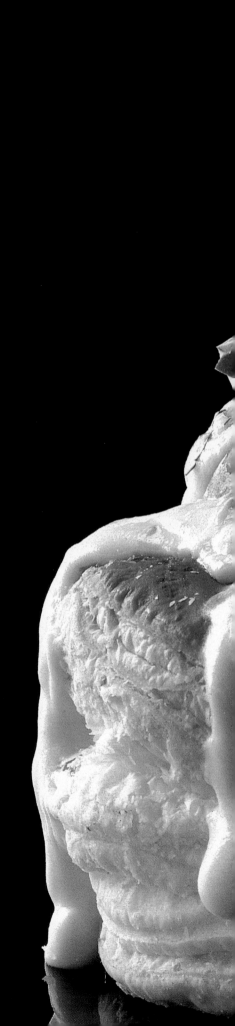

Frogs' Legs with Wine and Cream

Level of Difficulty	🍴🍴
Preparation Time	15 min
Cost per Serving	$ $
Number of Servings	6
Nutritional Value	190 calories 17 g protein 11 g lipids
Food Exchanges	2 oz meat 2 fat exchanges
Cooking Time	13 min
Standing Time	None
Power Level	100%, 70%
Write Your Cooking Time Here	

Ingredients
24 frogs' legs
50 mL (1/4 cup) butter
1 green onion, sliced
2 cloves garlic, chopped
50 mL (1/4 cup) white wine
125 mL (1/2 cup) 18% cream
5 mL (1 teaspoon) cornstarch
30 mL (2 tablespoons) cold water
5 mL (1 teaspoon) parsley, chopped
salt and pepper to taste

Method
— Preheat a browning dish at 100% for 7 minutes; add the butter and heat at 100% for 30 seconds.
— Sear the frogs' legs on all sides and add the green onion and garlic.
— Reduce the power to 70% and continue to cook for 7 to 9 minutes, stirring halfway through the cooking time.
— Remove the frogs' legs and arrange on a platter; cover and set aside.
— Pour the wine and the cream into the browning dish and mix well.
— Cook at 100% for 2 to 3 minutes, or until the mixture is very hot.
— Dissolve the cornstarch in the water, add to the sauce and cook at 100% for 1 minute, beating with a whisk halfway through the cooking time.
— Add the parsley, season to taste and pour the sauce over the frogs' legs before serving.

These are the ingredients needed to prepare this delicious recipe, which is sure to please all your guests.

Sear the frogs' legs on all sides in a preheated browning dish and then add the green onion and garlic.

Remove the frogs' legs, set aside and pour the wine and cream into the browning dish. Mix well and cook at 100% until the mixture is very hot.

Eggplant Ragout
with Lobster Tails

Level of Difficulty	🍴🍴
Preparation Time	20 min
Cost per Serving	$ $ $
Number of Servings	4
Nutritional Value	155 calories 10.9 g protein 5.3 g carbohydrate
Food Exchanges	1.5 oz meat 1 vegetable exchange 1 fat exchange
Cooking Time	16 min
Standing Time	None
Power Level	100%, 70%, 50%
Write Your Cooking Time Here	

Ingredients
225 g (8 oz) eggplant, cubed
4 small lobster tails
50 mL (1/4 cup) celery, thinly sliced
50 mL (1/4 cup) onion, finely chopped
50 mL (1/4 cup) water
30 mL (2 tablespoons) vinegar
5 mL (1 teaspoon) sugar
15 mL (1 tablespoon) oil
30 mL (2 tablespoons) butter
15 mL (1 tablespoon) capers
salt and pepper to taste
4 wooden skewers

Method
— Put the eggplant, celery and onion into a dish and add the water; cover and cook at 100% for 4 to 6 minutes.
— Drain and set aside.
— Combine the vinegar and sugar, pour over the mixture of cooked vegetables and set aside.
— Shell the lobster tails.
— Slide a wooden skewer lengthwise into each of the lobster tails.
— Cut off that part of the skewer protruding from each lobster tail.
— Preheat a browning dish at 100% for 7 minutes, pour in the oil and butter and heat at 100% for 30 seconds.
— Sear the lobster tails on each side.
— Reduce the power to 70% and cook for 4 to 6 minutes, moving the tails

in the center of the dish to the outside and vice-versa halfway through the cooking time.
— Put the vegetables into a microwave-save serving platter and arrange the lobster tails over them.
— Heat the dish at 50% for 3 to 4 minutes.
— Season and garnish with the capers before serving.

These are the ingredients needed to prepare this superb recipe. The delicate flavor of this combination is sure to charm the most exacting guests.

Put the eggplant, celery and onions into a dish. Add the water and cook at 100% for 4 to 6 minutes.

Zucchini Stuffed with Veal

Level of Difficulty	🍴🍴
Preparation Time	20 min
Cost per Serving	$
Number of Servings	4
Nutritional Value	152 calories 13.7 g protein 8.6 g carbohydrate
Food Exchanges	1.5 oz meat 2 vegetable exchanges
Cooking Time	13 min
Standing Time	3 min
Power Level	100%
Write Your Cooking Time Here	

MICROTIPS

Other Fillings for Zucchini

Zucchini pulp blends well with most stuffing ingredients, and the zucchini itself makes an attractive case for them. Instead of the ground veal used in the recipe below, try adding beaten egg yolks to the stuffing just before the final cooking stage. All kinds of variations are possible!

Ingredients
2 zucchini
225 g (8 oz) ground veal
50 mL (1/4 cup) onion, finely chopped
1 clove garlic, finely chopped
50 mL (1/4 cup) tomato sauce
5 mL (1 teaspoon) parsley, chopped
2 mL (1/2 teaspoon) oregano
salt and pepper to taste
50 mL (1/4 cup) breadcrumbs

Method
— Put the onion and garlic in a dish and cook at 100% for 2 minutes.
— Add the ground veal and continue to cook at 100% for 4 to 5 minutes, breaking the meat up with a fork halfway through the cooking time and again at the end; set aside.
— Cut the zucchini in half lengthwise and remove the pulp, leaving a 0.5 cm (1/4 inch) layer lining the skin on the inside.
— Chop the zucchini pulp and add the meat mixture, tomato sauce, parsley and oregano; mix well and season to taste.
— Stuff the zucchini with the mixture and sprinkle with the breadcrumbs.
— Put the zucchini in a baking dish; cover and cook at 100% for 4 to 6 minutes, or until the zucchini is cooked, giving the dish a half-turn halfway through the cooking time.
— Let stand for 3 minutes before serving.

Mixed Vegetables

Level of Difficulty	(utensils icon)
Preparation Time	20 min
Cost per Serving	**$**
Number of Servings	8
Nutritional Value	124 calories 12.4 g carbohydrate 6.8 g lipids
Food Exchanges	2 vegetable exchanges 1-1/2 fat exchanges
Cooking Time	22 min
Standing Time	3 min
Power Level	100%
Write Your Cooking Time Here	(apple and pencil icon)

Ingredients
250 mL (1 cup) carrots, finely sliced
50 mL (1/4 cup) water
500 mL (2 cups) broccoli flowerets
500 mL (2 cups) corn
500 mL (2 cups) cauliflower flowerets
50 mL (1/4 cup) butter
2 mL (1/2 teaspoon) rosemary
15 mL (1 tablespoon) red pepper, roasted and chopped
50 mL (1/4 cup) Parmesan cheese, grated

Method
— Put the carrots in a dish, add the water and cook covered at 100% for 7 minutes, stirring after 4 minutes.
— Add the broccoli, corn and cauliflower; cover and continue to cook at 100% for 10 to 12 minutes, or until the vegetables are cooked, stirring once during the cooking time.
— Drain the vegetables, cover and let stand for 3 minutes.
— In another dish, melt the butter at 100% for 1 minute, add the rosemary and red pepper and mix well.
— Pour the seasoned butter over the vegetables and sprinkle with the Parmesan.
— Heat through at 100% for 2 minutes.

The secret of this flavorful dish lies in the interesting combination of vegetables. First assemble all the necessary ingredients.

40

Put the carrots and water into a dish, cover and cook at 100% for 7 minutes.

Add the broccoli, corn and cauliflower. Cover and continue to cook at 100% for 10 to 12 minutes.

Drain the vegetables, return them to the dish and let stand, covered, for 3 minutes before continuing with the next step in the recipe.

Stuffed Vine Leaves

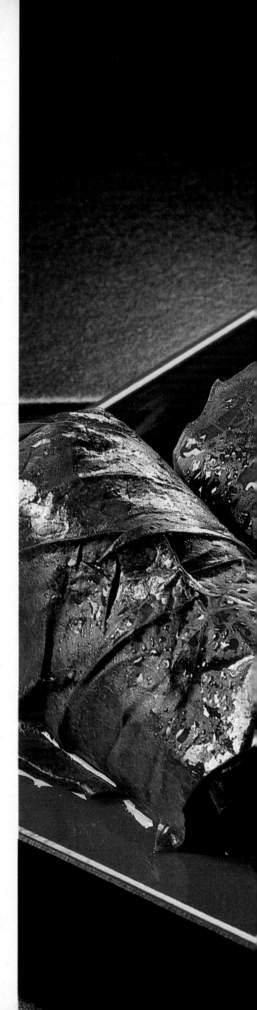

Level of Difficulty	🍴🍴
Preparation Time	20 min
Cost per Serving	$
Number of Servings	6
Nutritional Value	170 calories 15 g protein 8.3 g lipids
Food Exchanges	1.5 oz meat 1 vegetable exchange 1 fat exchange
Cooking Time	15 min
Standing Time	None
Power Level	100%, 70%
Write Your Cooking Time Here	

Ingredients

225 g (8 oz) vine leaves
45 mL (3 tablespoons) water
340 g (12 oz) ground veal
1 onion, finely chopped
125 mL (1/2 cup) rice, cooked
2 mL (1/2 teaspoon) paprika
2 mL (1/2 teaspoon) coriander
1 mL (1/4 teaspoon) cumin
1 mL (1/4 teaspoon) cayenne pepper
5 mL (1 teaspoon) rosemary
salt and pepper to taste
250 mL (1 cup) chicken broth
125 mL (1/2 cup) 18% cream
15 mL (1 tablespoon) cornstarch dissolved in 45 mL (3 tablespoons) cold water

Method

— To blanch the vine leaves put them in a dish, add the water, cover and cook at 100% for 2 to 3 minutes.
— Drain the vine leaves, dry and set aside.
— In a dish combine the veal, onion, rice, paprika, coriander, cumin, cayenne, rosemary, salt and pepper and mix well.
— Stuff each leaf with about 22 mL (1-1/2 tablespoons) of the mixture.
— Roll each leaf up and secure with a toothpick; arrange the leaves in a baking dish and pour the

Stuffed Vine Leaves

These are the ingredients you will need to prepare this dish, very reminiscent of Mediterranean cuisine.

First blanch the vine leaves by cooking them briefly in water in a covered dish.

Combine the ground veal, onion, rice, paprika, coriander, cumin, cayenne, rosemary, salt and pepper to make the stuffing.

Stuff the vine leaves, roll them up and secure with toothpicks.

Place the vine leaves in a dish and add the chicken broth.

Halfway through the cooking time, rearrange the stuffed vine leaves, moving those in the center of the dish toward the outside.

chicken broth over them.
— Cover the dish and cook at 100% for 5 minutes.
— Reduce the power to 70% and continue to cook for 3 to 4 minutes, moving the leaves from the center of

the dish to the outside halfway through the cooking time.
— Remove the vine leaves, cover and set aside.
— Add the cream and the dissolved cornstarch to

the cooking liquid and season to taste.
— Cook at 100% for 2 to 3 minutes, beating with a wire whisk every minute.
— Pour the sauce over the vine leaves and serve.

Spicy Frankfurters

Ingredients
450 g (1 lb) frankfurters, cut into bit-sized pieces
60 mL (4 tablespoons) onion, grated

1 green pepper, finely chopped
1 red pepper, finely chopped
1 clove garlic, finely chopped
250 mL (1 cup) tomato juice

5 mL (1 teaspoon) sugar
5 mL (1 teaspoon) Worcestershire sauce
2 mL (1/2 teaspoon) Tabasco sauce
2 mL (1/2 teaspoon) cayenne pepper
salt and pepper to taste
15 mL (1 tablespoon) cornstarch dissolved in 50 mL (1/4 cup) cold water

Level of Difficulty	🍴
Preparation Time	20 min
Cost per Serving	$
Number of Servings	8
Nutritional Value	189 calories 6.8 g protein 4.4 g carbohydrate
Food Exchanges	1 oz meat 1 vegetable exchange 2 fat exchanges
Cooking Time	19 min
Standing Time	None
Power Level	100%
Write Your Cooking Time Here	

Method
— Put the onion, peppers and garlic into a dish; cover and cook at 100% for 3 minutes.
— Add the tomato juice, sugar, Worcestershire, Tabasco and the seasonings; cover and cook at 100% for 9 minutes, stirring halfway through the cooking time.
— Add the dissolved cornstarch; mix well and cook at 100% for 1 to 2 minutes, stirring once.
— Add the frankfurters; cover and cook at 100% for 3 to 5 minutes, stirring once.

Mini Chicken Kebabs

Level of Difficulty	 🍴🍴
Preparation Time	20 min*
Cost per Serving	**$**
Number of Servings	8
Nutritional Value	124 calories 12 g protein 9.1 g carbohydrate
Food Exchanges	1.5 oz meat 1 vegetable exchange
Cooking Time	12 min
Standing Time	3 min
Power Level	70%
Write Your Cooking Time Here	

* The chicken must be marinated for 1 hour before cooking.

Ingredients
2 whole chicken breasts, cut in half
1 green pepper, cut into 8 pieces
8 mushrooms
8 small white onions
8 cherry tomatoes
16 wooden skewers, 12 cm (5 in) long

Marinade:
75 mL (1/3 cup) lemon juice
1 clove garlic, finely chopped
2 onions, finely chopped
30 mL (2 tablespoons) oil
50 mL (1/4 cup) soy sauce
2 mL (1/2 teaspoon) pepper
5 mL (1 teaspoon) salt
pinch thyme
2 mL (1/2 teaspoon) basil

Method
— Combine all the marinade ingredients in a dish and mix well.
— Bone and skin the chicken breasts and cut into 32 cubes of equal size.
— Put the chicken cubes into the marinade and let stand for 1 hour at room temperature, stirring several times.
— Thread the chicken cubes onto wooden skewers, alternating with the vegetables, placing the cherry tomatoes at the center of the skewers.
— Brush the skewers with the marinade and place them on a dish, their ends suspended over the sides of the dish.
— Cook at 70% for 10 to 12 minutes, basting them with the marinade and moving the center skewers to the ends of the dish every 3 minutes.
— Cover and let stand for 3 minutes before serving.

46

These are the ingredients required to make these delicious chicken kebabs.

Marinate the chicken cubes for 1 hour so that they absorb all the flavor of the marinade.

After assembling the skewers baste them with the marinade and begin the cooking.

Ham Rolls

Level of Difficulty	
Preparation Time	15 min
Cost per Serving	$
Number of Servings	8
Nutritional Value	241 calories 10.1 g protein 19.4 g lipids
Food Exchanges	1 oz meat 3 fat exchanges 1/4 bread exchange 1/2 milk exchange
Cooking Time	8 min
Standing Time	2 min
Power Level	100%, 70%
Write Your Cooking Time Here	

Ingredients
8 slices cooked ham
8 broccoli stalks
30 mL (2 tablespoons) water
125 mL (1/2 cup) mayonnaise
45 mL (3 tablespoons) flour
2 mL (1/2 teaspoon) salt
pepper to taste
375 mL (1-1/2 cups) milk
50 mL (1/4 cup) Parmesan
cheese, grated
75 mL (1/3) breadcrumbs

Method
— Put the broccoli into a dish and add the water; cover and cook at 100% for 3 minutes, (the broccoli should still be firm), stirring once halfway through the cooking time.
— Drain and set aside.
— In a bowl, combine the mayonnaise, flour, salt and pepper and add the milk gradually, beating constantly with a wire whisk; set aside.
— Place one broccoli stalk on each slice of ham; roll up the ham and secure with toothpicks.
— Place the rolls in a dish and add the prepared sauce.
— Sprinkle with the grated Parmesan and the breadcrumbs.
— Cook uncovered at 70% for 3 to 5 minutes, giving the dish a half-turn after 2 minutes of cooking.
— Let stand for 2 minutes before serving.

Pictured here are the ingredients you will need to prepare these popular ham rolls.

Place a broccoli stalk on each slice of ham, roll up and secure with a toothpick.

Sprinkle with the grated Parmesan and breadcrumbs before cooking.

Artichoke Bottoms with Two Stuffings

Level of Difficulty	🍴🍴
Preparation Time	30 min
Cost per Serving	$ $
Number of Servings	6
Nutritional Value	219 calories 13.3 g carbohydrate 14.6 g lipids
Food Exchanges	2 vegetable exchanges 3-1/2 fat exchanges
Cooking Time	18 min
Standing Time	None
Power Level	100%
Write Your Cooking Time Here	

Ingredients
12 artichoke bottoms
125 mL (1/2 cup) Parmesan cheese, grated
5 mL (1 teaspoon) paprika

Spinach Stuffing:
450 g (1 lb) spinach
50 mL (1/4 cup) butter, melted
50 mL (1/4 cup) 18% cream
pinch nutmeg
salt and pepper to taste

Mushroom Stuffing:
225 g (8 oz) mushrooms, chopped
1 clove garlic, chopped
2 green onion, chopped

Béchamel Sauce:
10 mL (2 teaspoons) butter
10 mL (2 teaspoons) flour
125 mL (1/2 cup) milk
salt and pepper to taste

Method
— To prepare the spinach stuffing, rinse the spinach well and chop; cook at 100% for 4 to 5 minutes, stirring halfway through the cooking time.
— Remove the spinach and drain well by squeezing it with your hands; return the spinach to the dish and add the remaining spinach stuffing ingredients; mix well and set aside.

Artichoke Bottoms with Two Stuffings

This delicious spinach stuffing is very easy to prepare. First assemble all the ingredients.

Cook the spinach and drain by squeezing it with you hands.

Put the spinach into a bowl and add the other ingredients, mixing well.

Your guests are also bound to enjoy the mushroom stuffing. First assemble the ingredients required.

Combine the mushrooms, garlic and green onion in a dish; cover and cook for 3 to 4 minutes at 100%.

Drain the mushroom mixture in a sieve, before preparing the béchamel sauce.

— Next, prepare the mushroom stuffing by combining the three ingredients in a dish; mix well, cover and cook at 100% for 3 to 4 minutes.
— Place the mixture in a sieve, drain and set aside.
— To make the béchamel, melt the butter in a dish at 100% for 30 seconds, add the flour and mix well.

— Add the milk, beat with a whisk and season.
— Cook at 100% for 2 to 3 minutes, whisking twice during the cooking time.
— Add the béchamel sauce to the mushroom stuffing, mix well and season to taste.
— Fill 6 artichoke bottoms with the spinach stuffing and the remaining 6 with

the mushroom stuffing; sprinkle with the Parmesan and paprika.
— Arrange the artichoke bottoms in a dish and place on a raised rack in the oven; cook at 100% for 4 to 6 minutes, giving the dish a half-turn halfway through the cooking time.

Stuffed Cucumbers

Ingredients
2 cucumbers, 450 g (1 lb) each
225 g (8 oz) sausage meat
125 mL (1/2 cup) hot chicken broth
5 mL (1 teaspoon) cornstarch
30 mL (2 tablespoons) cold water
salt and pepper to taste

Level of Difficulty	🍴 🍴
Preparation Time	15 min
Cost per Serving	**$**
Number of Servings	4
Nutritional Value	236 calories 9.4 g protein 18.8 g lipids
Food Exchanges	1.5 oz meat 1 vegetable exchange 2 fat exchanges
Cooking Time	18 min
Standing Time	None
Power Level	70%, 100%
Write Your Cooking Time Here	

Method
— Cut the cucumbers in two, lengthwise. Scoop out the seeds and discard. Hollow out the pulp, leaving a 0.5 cm (1/4 inch) layer of pulp lining the skin.
— Fill the cucumbers with sausage meat.
— Put the cucumbers in a dish with the broth; cook uncovered at 70% for 14 to 16 minutes, moving the cucumbers from the center of the dish to the outside halfway through the cooking time.
— Remove the cucumbers from the dish and set aside, covered.
— Dissolve the cornstarch in the water and add it to the broth. Season to taste.
— Cook at 100% for 1 to 2 minutes; stir with a whisk halfway through the cooking time and again at the end.
— Pour the sauce over the cucumbers and serve immediately.

Asparagus with Mornay or Béarnaise Sauce

Level of Difficulty	🍴🍴
Preparation Time	20 min
Cost per Serving	$ $
Number of Servings	10
Nutritional Value	172 calories 15.3 g lipids
Food Exchanges	1 vegetable exchange 3 fat exchanges
Cooking Time	14 to 16 min
Standing Time	None
Power Level	100%
Write Your Cooking Time Here	

Ingredients
900 g (2 lb) asparagus
50 mL (1/4 cup) water

Mornay Sauce:
10 mL (2 tablespoons) butter
10 mL (2 tablespoons) flour
125 mL (1/2 cup) milk
salt and pepper to taste
1 egg yolk
50 mL (1/4 cup) 18% cream
50 mL (1/4 cup) cheddar
cheese, grated

Béarnaise Sauce:
4 egg yolks
10 mL (2 teaspoons) white
vinegar
5 mL (1 teaspoon) dried onion
flakes
5 mL (1 teaspoon) tarragon
2 mL (1/2 teaspoon) chervil
125 mL (1/2 cup) butter
5 mL (1 teaspoon) fresh
parsley, chopped

Method
— Put the asparagus in a dish
  and add the water.
— Cover and cook at 100%
  for 10 to 12 minutes, or
  until the asparagus is done
  to your liking.
— Drain and set aside.
— Serve the asparagus with
  mornay or béarnaise
  sauce.

Mornay Sauce:
— First prepare a béchamel
  sauce.
— Melt the butter in a dish at
  100% for 30 seconds.
— Add the flour and mix
  well.
— Add the milk, beating with
  a whisk and season to
  taste.
— Cook at 100% for 2 to 3
  minutes, beating with the
  whisk twice during the
  cooking time; set aside.
— In a bowl, combine the egg
  yolk and the cream and
  add 30 mL (2 tablespoons)
  of the warm béchamel
  sauce.
— Add this mixture to the
  remaining béchamel, add
  the cheddar and stir
  constantly until the cheese
  has melted.
— Heat at 100% for 1 minute
  and serve with the
  asparagus immediately.

Béarnaise Sauce:
— Put the egg yolks, vinegar,
  onions, tarragon and
  chervil into a blender.
— Melt the butter at 100%
  for 1 to 2 minutes, or until
  bubbling very gently.
— Blend the ingredients in
  the blender at high speed
  and add the butter, very
  slowly, through the top
  opening until the sauce is
  thick and creamy.
— Pour the sauce into a
  bowl, sprinkle with
  parsley and serve with the
  asparagus immediately.

Carrots Basque

Level of Difficulty	 (icon)
Preparation Time	20 min
Cost per Serving	$
Number of Servings	4
Nutritional Value	180 calories 10.3 g protein 14.3 g carbohydrate
Food Exchanges	1 oz meat 1 vegetable exchange 2 fat exchanges
Cooking Time	13 min
Standing Time	3 min
Power Level	100%
Write Your Cooking Time Here	

Ingredients
450 g (1 lb) carrots
75 mL (1/3 cup) water
1 onion, chopped
2 cloves garlic, crushed
30 mL (2 tablespoons) oil
115 g (4 oz) ham, cut into cubes
15 mL (1 tablespoon) vinegar
15 mL (1 tablespoon) lemon juice
5 mL (1 teaspoon) parsley, chopped
salt and pepper, to taste

Method
— Cut the carrots into thin round slices, put them in a dish and add the water.
— Cover and cook at 100% for 7 to 9 minutes.
— Let stand for 3 minutes, drain and set aside, covered.
— Put the onion and garlic in a dish and add the oil; cook at 100% for 2 minutes.
— Add the cubes of ham and cook at 100% for 2 minutes.
— Pour the mixture over the carrots and set aside.
— In a bowl, combine the vinegar, lemon juice, parsley, salt and pepper; mix well, pour over the carrots and serve immediately.

Carrots in the Basque tradition make a simple dish that is always appreciated. First assemble the ingredients required.

Cook the carrots with the water in a covered dish.

Add the cubes of ham to the onion and garlic mixture.

Potatoes Stuffed with Sardines

Level of Difficulty	🍴🍴
Preparation Time	20 min
Cost per Serving	$
Number of Servings	6
Nutritional Value	290 calories 11.9 g protein 23.7 g carbohydrate 20.4 g lipids
Food Exchanges	1.5 oz meat 1 bread exchange 2 fat exchanges
Cooking Time	17 min
Standing Time	3 min
Power Level	100%, 70%
Write Your Cooking Time Here	

Ingredients
6 large potatoes, washed but not peeled
175 mL (3/4 cup) milk
50 mL (1/4 cup) green onions, chopped
50 mL (1/4 cup) butter
15 mL (1 tablespoon) parsley, chopped
125 mL (1/2 cup) cheddar cheese, grated
salt and pepper to taste
284 g (10 oz) sardines
6 slices of bacon, crisply cooked and crumbled

Method
— Pierce each potato skin in several places with a fork.
— Put the potatoes in a dish and cook at 100% for 10 to 12 minutes, giving the dish a half-turn after 6 minutes of cooking.
— Slice a thin layer off the top of each potato.
— Hollow out the potatoes, leaving a 0.5 cm (1/4 inch) layer of pulp lining the skin on the inside.
— In a bowl, mash the potato pulp and add the milk, green onions, butter, parsley, cheese, salt and pepper; mix well.
— Flake the sardines and add to the potato pulp, mixing well.
— Stuff each potato skin with the mixture.
— Sprinkle with the bacon bits.
— Put the stuffed potatoes into a dish and heat through at 70% for 4 to 5

minutes, giving the dish a
half-turn halfway through
the cooking time.
— Let stand for 3 minutes
before serving.

MICROTIPS

Cleaning the Cheese Grater

If fragments of cheese
are left in the cheese
grater after use, they will
dry out and become
hard. The grater will
then be very difficult to
clean, even with hot
water. You can avoid
this problem by soaking
the grater in a bowl of
tepid water before
washing it.

Potatoes Stuffed with Sardines

All your guests will enjoy these stuffed potatoes. First assemble the ingredients required for the recipe.

Hollow out the potatoes, leaving a 0.5 cm (1/4 inch) layer of pulp lining the inside.

Spoon the prepared filling into the potato skins, garnish with the bacon bits and heat through.

MICROTIPS

Cooking with Onions

An excellent aromatic, the onion is one of the most flavorful vegetables and, without doubt, one of the vegetables most used in the kitchen. Onions can be cooked in many different ways with many different foods and, as they blend well with all of them, the resulting dishes are always pleasing.

Baked Onions? Why Not?

Potatoes are not the only vegetable that taste great when baked. Try cooking onions in their skins in the microwave and serve them with a bit of butter. Have your guests cut into their own onions and enjoy the dramatic impact of the wonderful aroma.

If Onions Make You Cry . . .

Do your eyes sting and water when you peel onions? There are ways of minimizing these disagreeable effects. Try peeling them in front of a window that is wide open in the summer or immersing them in cold water before peeling and chopping them in the winter.

Keeping Your Friends While Enjoying Onions

Onions are delicious whether eaten raw or lightly cooked but, unfortunately, they can leave a somewhat disagreeable odor on your breath. But don't worry, there is an antidote—a miracle naturally produced called parsley.

Cleaning Your Knife After Slicing Onions

To get rid of any odor that may linger on your knife after slicing or chopping onions, simply run the blade through a raw potato.

Vegetables au Gratin

Ingredients
4 potatoes, thinly sliced
50 mL (1/4 cup) onion, finely chopped
75 mL (1/3 cup) water
250 mL (1 cup) zucchini, thinly sliced

50 mL (1/4 cup) butter
30 mL (2 tablespoons) flour
125 mL (1/2 cup) milk
salt, pepper and paprika to taste
2 tomatoes, chopped
30 mL (2 tablespoons) butter, melted

50 mL (1/4 cup) Parmesan cheese, grated
50 mL (1/4 cup) seasoned breadcrumbs

Level of Difficulty	🍴
Preparation Time	20 min
Cost per Serving	$
Number of Servings	8
Nutritional Value	177 calories 17.8 g carbohydrate 10 g lipids
Food Exchanges	1 vegetable exchange 1 bread exchange 1-1/2 fat exchanges
Cooking Time	15 min
Standing Time	3 min
Power Level	100%
Write Your Cooking Time Here	

Method
— Put the potatoes, onions and water in a dish; cover and cook at 100% for 4 to 5 minutes.
— Add the zucchini and cook at 100% for 2 minutes longer. Set aside.
— Melt the 50 mL (1/4 cup) butter in a dish at 100% for 1 minute; add the flour and mix well.
— Heat the milk at 100% for 1 to 2 minutes and add to the butter and flour, mixing well.
— Season and set aside.
— Drain the cooked vegetables, add the tomatoes and then the sauce.
— Combine the melted butter, Parmesan and breadcrumbs and top the vegetables with this mixture.
— Cook uncovered at 100% for 4 to 5 minutes.
— Allow to stand for 3 minutes before serving.

Tomatoes Stuffed with Rice

Level of Difficulty	
Preparation Time	20 min
Cost per Serving	$
Number of Servings	6
Nutritional Value	133 calories 16.2 g carbohydrate 5.2 g lipids
Food Exchanges	2 vegetable exchanges 1/2 bread exchange 1 fat exchange
Cooking Time	18 min
Standing Time	None
Power Level	100%, 70%
Write Your Cooking Time Here	

Ingredients
6 large tomatoes
125 mL (1/2 cup) long grain rice
250 mL (1 cup) hot vegetable bouillon
30 mL (2 tablespoons) butter
125 mL (1/2 cup) onion, finely chopped
50 mL (1/4 cup) green pepper, finely chopped
salt and pepper to taste
30 mL (2 tablespoons) Italian breadcrumbs
50 mL (1/4 cup) Parmesan cheese, grated

Method
— Pour the vegetable bouillon into a dish and add the rice; cover and cook at 100% for 3 minutes.
— Reduce the power to 70% and cook for 5 to 7 minutes, or until the rice is cooked, and set aside.
— Put the butter in a dish and add the onion and the green pepper; cook at 100% for 3 to 4 minutes, stirring halfway through the cooking time.
— Add the cooked vegetables to the rice and mix well; season to taste and set aside.
— Cut a thin slice off the top of each tomato and set the slices aside.
— Hollow out some of the tomato pulp, leaving enough inside so that the tomatoes hold their shape. Add the pulp to the vegetables and rice and mix well.
— Stuff the tomatoes with the mixture of vegetables and rice.
— Combine the breadcrumbs and the Parmesan and

sprinkle over the stuffed
tomatoes.
— Put the tomatoes in a dish
  and cook at 100% for 4
  minutes, giving the dish a
  half-turn halfway through
  the cooking time.
— Put the slices that were
  removed back on top of
  each tomato, to form lids,
  and serve.

*Here are the ingredients you
will need to prepare these
stuffed tomatoes, a side dish
that will add distinction to any
meal.*

MICROTIPS

Embellishing Fruits and Vegetables

Fruits and vegetables can
be decoratively cut in
many ways to make
attractive presentations.
Try cutting the tops of
tomatoes with jagged
edges, cutting oranges
and lemons into baskets
and cucumbers into star
shapes.

Eggplant and Tomato Fricassee

Level of Difficulty	🍴🍴
Preparation Time	20 min*
Cost per Serving	**$**
Number of Servings	8
Nutritional Value	68 calories 12.1 g carbohydrate
Food Exchanges	2 vegetable exchanges
Cooking Time	14 min
Standing Time	3 min
Power Level	100%
Write Your Cooking Time Here	

* After adding the salt, leave the eggplant slices to sweat for 30 to 45 minutes before cooking them.

Ingredients
2 large eggplants
coarse salt
1 Spanish onion, chopped
15 mL (1 tablespoon) butter
1 540 mL (19 oz) can tomatoes, drained and chopped
2 mL (1/2 teaspoon) basil
pepper to taste

Method
— Peel and cut the eggplant into slices and sprinkle them with coarse salt.
— Leave the slices to sweat, drawing out excess moisture, for 30 to 45 minutes and then rinse well with cold water; drain and pat dry.
— Put the eggplant and onion in a dish, add the butter and cook at 100% for 8 to 10 minutes, stirring halfway through the cooking time.
— Add the tomatoes, basil and pepper.
— Cook at 100% for 3 to 4 minutes.
— Let stand for 3 minutes before serving.

Eggplant lovers will particularly enjoy this recipe. First assemble the ingredients required.

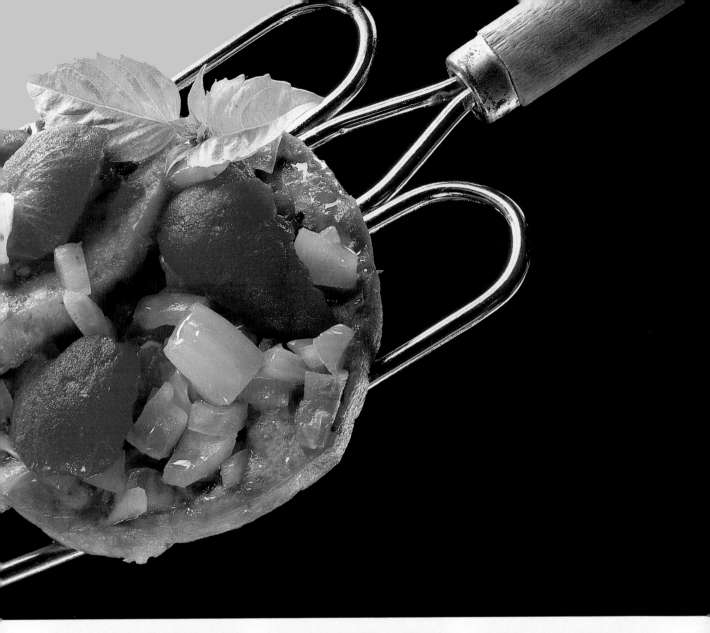

Cut the eggplant into uniform slices and sprinkle them with coarse salt.

Before cooking, the eggplant must be left to sweat for 30 to 45 minutes to extract the excess moisture.

After cooking the onion and the eggplant, add the tomatoes and basil and season to taste. Continue to cook at 100% for 3 to 4 minutes.

Festive Summer Vegetables

Level of Difficulty	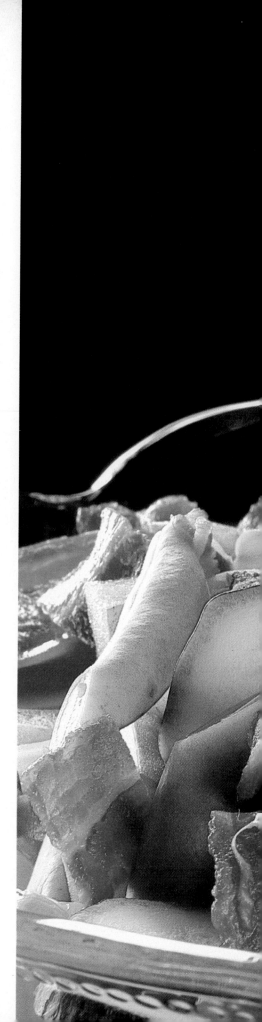
Preparation Time	20 min
Cost per Serving	$
Number of Servings	8
Nutritional Value	61 calories 8.8 g carbohydrate
Food Exchanges	2 vegetable exchanges 1/2 fat exchange
Cooking Time	20 min
Standing Time	5 min
Power Level	100%
Write Your Cooking Time Here	

Ingredients
4 slices of bacon
12 small white onions
1 green pepper, diced
75 mL (1/3 cup) water
15 mL (1 tablespoon) sugar
450 g (1 lb) green beans, cut into two
6 zucchini, finely sliced
2 celery stalks, chopped
1 large tomato, cut into quarters

Method
— Put the bacon on a rack and cover with paper towel to prevent splattering. Cook at 100% for 3 to 4 minutes, giving the rack a half-turn halfway through the cooking time.
— Crumble the bacon and set aside.
— Add the onions and green pepper to the bacon fat and cook at 100% for 3 to 4 minutes.
— Add the water and sugar and mix well.
— Add the green beans, zucchini and celery; cover and cook at 100% for 10 to 12 minutes, stirring halfway through the cooking time.
— Add the tomato quarters and stir gently.
— Let stand for 5 minutes.
— Arrange the cooked vegetables on a serving platter, sprinkle with the crumbled bacon and serve.

Stuffed Mushroom Caps

Level of Difficulty	🍴🍴
Preparation Time	25 min
Cost per Serving	$
Number of Servings	8
Nutritional Value	216 calories 11.5 g protein 14.7 g carbohydrate
Food Exchanges	1 oz meat 1-1/2 vegetable exchanges 1/2 bread exchange 1 fat exchange
Cooking Time	10 min
Standing Time	1 min
Power Level	100%
Write Your Cooking Time Here	

Ingredients
900 g (2 lb) large mushrooms
225 g (8 oz) sausage meat
3 green onions, chopped
3 cloves garlic, chopped
5 mL (1 teaspoon) chervil
2 egg yolks, beaten
15 mL (1 tablespoon) butter, melted
125 mL (1/2 cup) breadcrumbs

Method
— Clean the mushrooms with a vegetable brush and wipe with paper towel.
— Cut the stems off and chop finely; set the caps aside.
— Put the sausage meat in a dish, add the green onions and cook at 100% for 4 to 5 minutes, breaking up the meat with a fork once halfway through the cooking time and again at the end. Remove any fat.
— Add the chopped mushroom stems, garlic, chervil and egg yolks and mix well.
— Combine the melted butter and the breadcrumbs and set aside.
— Stuff the mushroom caps with the sausage meat mixture.
— Place the stuffed mushroom caps in a dish and sprinkle with the breadcrumbs and butter.
— Place the dish on a raised rack in the oven and cook at 100% for 4 to 5 minutes, giving the dish a half-turn halfway through the cooking time.
— Let stand for 1 minute before serving.

Stuffed mushroom caps are always suitable—for small gatherings or large celebrations. These are the ingredients required to make this recipe.

Break up the sausage meat with a fork halfway through the cooking time and once again at the end of it.

Stuff the mushroom caps with the sausage meat mixture.

Cabbage Au Gratin

Level of Difficulty	🍴
Preparation Time	20 min
Cost per Serving	**$**
Number of Servings	8
Nutritional Value	188 calories 6.3 g protein 12 g lipids
Food Exchanges	0.5 oz meat 2 vegetable exchanges 2 fat exchanges
Cooking Time	14 min
Standing Time	3 min
Power Level	100%
Write Your Cooking Time Here	

Ingredients
1 large green cabbage
60 mL (4 tablespoons) butter
30 mL (2 tablespoons) flour
250 mL (1 cup) 10% cream
salt and pepper to taste
5 mL (1 teaspoon) dry
mustard
pinch nutmeg
125 mL (1/2 cup) orange
cheddar cheese, grated
50 mL (1/4 cup) Parmesan
cheese, grated

Method
— Slice the cabbage into thin strips.
— Put the cabbage in a dish and add half the butter; cover and cook at 100% for 5 to 6 minutes, stirring halfway through the cooking time.
— Let stand for 3 minutes, drain in a sieve and set aside.
— Put the remaining butter in a dish and melt at 100% for 30 seconds; add the flour and mix well.
— Add the cream, beating with a whisk, and season to taste; cook at 100% for 3 to 4 minutes, stirring twice during the cooking time.
— Add the mustard and nutmeg and whisk again to mix well.
— Combine the cheddar and the Parmesan and set aside.
— Line a pie plate with the cooked cabbage and pour the sauce over it.
— Sprinkle with the grated cheese mixture and cook at 100% for 3 to 4 minutes, giving the dish a half-turn halfway through the cooking time.

Cut the cabbage into thin strips before cooking it.

Beat the sauce well with a wire whisk twice during the cooking time.

Pour the sauce over the cooked cabbage and sprinkle with the mixture of cheddar and Parmesan cheeses before the final cooking stage.

71

Cauliflower Quiche

Level of Difficulty	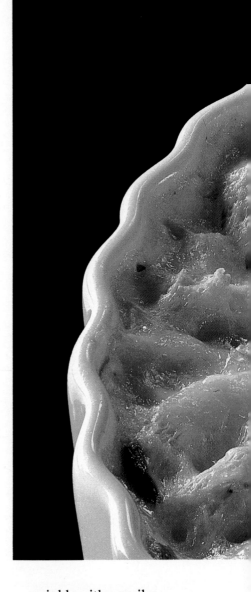
Preparation Time	10 min
Cost per Serving	$
Number of Servings	6
Nutritional Value	164 calories 11.9 g protein 11.1 g carbohydrate
Food Exchanges	1 oz meat 1 vegetable exchange 1/2 fat exchange 1/4 milk exchange
Cooking Time	10 min
Standing Time	3 min
Power Level	100%
Write Your Cooking Time Here	

Ingredients
1 cauliflower
2 green onions, chopped
500 mL (2 cups) milk
4 eggs, beaten
15 mL (1 tablespoon) flour
salt and pepper to taste
125 mL (1/2 cup) Gruyère
cheese, grated
paprika to garnish

Method
— Trim the cauliflower, separate it into flowerets and arrange in a quiche dish.
— Sprinkle the chopped green onions over the cauliflower.
— In a bowl, combine the milk, eggs, flour, salt and pepper; mix well and pour over the vegetables.
— Top with the Gruyère and sprinkle with paprika.
— Place on a raised rack in the oven and cook at 100% for 8 to 10 minutes, giving the dish a half-turn halfway through the cooking time.
— Let stand for 3 minutes before serving.

Trim the cauliflower, separate it into flowerets and place them in the quiche dish.

Combine the milk, eggs, flour, salt and pepper; mix well and pour over the vegetables.

Add the Gruyère and sprinkle with paprika before putting the quiche in the oven.

Corn—Always Delicious!

Did you know that it was Christopher Columbus who, on his first voyage to this continent, discovered corn? The Italian explorer thought he had finally found the passage to the East from where he had hoped to bring back a multitude of treasures. But instead of precious gems, ears of corn filled the coffers of his boat on its return to Europe.

Corn originated in South America but is now cultivated in several parts of the world. It is very popular for human consumption, especially in America, but is used to feed animals as well.

Corn, although mainly consumed during the summer months, is available all year round. It contains carbohydrates, proteins and many vitamins. Cooking corn in the microwave oven takes advantage of all these nutritional qualities because no water is needed; all the water soluble vitamins as well as the corn's attractive yellow color are therefore preserved.

Corn is best kept in a cool location since heat accelerates the transformation of sugar into starch. If pinching a kernel reveals a milky white liquid, you can be assured that the corn is fresh and crisp.

Corn is particularly well suited to microwave cooking. We suggest that you leave the cob encased in its surrounding leaves to better preserve its natural flavor. One ear of fresh corn requires 2 to 4 minutes cooking time at 100% power and 1 minute standing time following the cooking. Each additional cob requires an extra 1 to 2 minutes cooking time. The water used to clean the corn prior to cooking provides enough moisture for it to cook without risk of drying out. Corn should be cooked covered, using a lid or plastic wrap, to retain the moisture.

Corn on the cob is considered to be rather heavy and is therefore not an appropriate item to serve as an appetizer. It does, however, make an excellent side dish, especially at the height of its season— with barbecued steak, for instance, and at all those fine summer evening get-togethers!

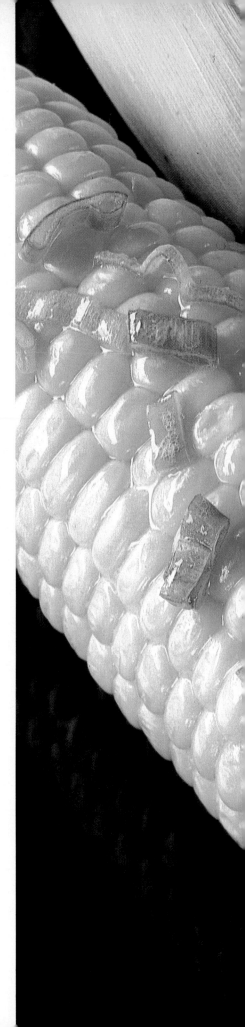

Eggplant with Cream

Level of Difficulty	
Preparation Time	20 min*
Cost per Serving	$
Number of Servings	8
Nutritional Value	141 calories 10.8 g lipids
Food Exchanges	2 vegetable exchanges 2 fat exchanges
Cooking Time	8 min
Standing Time	None
Power Level	100%, 90%
Write Your Cooking Time Here	

* After adding the salt, leave the eggplants to sweat for 30 minutes before cooking.

Ingredients
900 g (2 lb) eggplant
coarse salt
50 mL (1/4 cup) butter
1 clove garlic, chopped
250 mL (1 cup) 18% cream
15 mL (1 tablespoon) parsley, chopped
salt and pepper to taste
pinch nutmeg

Method
— Cut the eggplants into uniform slices and sprinkle with coarse salt.
— Allow the slices to sweat for 30 minutes and then rinse well under cold water; drain and pat dry.
— Preheat a browning dish at 100% for 7 minutes; add the butter and heat at 100% for 30 seconds.
— Sear the eggplant slices, add the garlic and cook at 100% for 4 to 5 minutes.
— In the meantime, combine the cream, parsley, salt, pepper and nutmeg in a bowl and pour over the eggplant.
— Reduce the power to 90% and continue to cook for 2 to 3 minutes, stirring once during the cooking time.

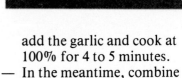

MICROTIPS

About Sauces: Classic Combinations

Here are some well-known sauces and the foods they most frequently accompany to make traditionally classic combinations.

Roux-based sauces
Béchamel (vegetables, poultry, seafood)

Velouté (white meat, seafood)
Ravigote (cold meats, fish, chicken)

Egg-based sauces
Hollandaise (salmon, chicken, green vegetables)
Béarnaise (red meat, fish)
Mousseline (vegetables, poultry, fish, egg-based dishes)

Tomato-based sauces
Bolognese (spaghetti and pizza)
Provençale (red meat, fish, seafood)
Portugaise (fish)

Cream-based sauces
Allemande (poultry, fish, vegetables)
Mushroom (poultry and veal)
Supreme (meat, poultry, fish, vegetables)

Avocados with Cream Cheese and Nuts

Level of Difficulty	
Preparation Time	20 min
Cost per Serving	**$**
Number of Servings	4
Nutritional Value	412 calories 8.3 g protein 38.5 g lipids
Food Exchanges	1 oz meat 2 vegetable exchanges 6 fat exchanges
Cooking Time	1 min
Standing Time	None
Power Level	50%
Write Your Cooking Time Here	

Ingredients
2 avocados
lemon juice
175 g (6 oz) cream cheese
30 mL (2 tablespoons) milk
pepper to taste
125 mL (1/2 cup) walnuts,
chopped

Method
— Heat the cream cheese at
50% for 1 minute and add
the milk, pepper and
walnuts. Mix well and
chill.
— Just before serving, cut the
avocados lengthwise and
remove the seed.
— Brush the inside with
lemon juice to prevent
discoloration.
— Stuff the cavities left by
removing the seeds of the
avocados with the cheese
mixture and serve.

*Avocados are always a popular
appetizer. Try them stuffed
with this delightful mixture of
cream cheese, milk, pepper and
walnuts.*

MICROTIPS

**Keeping Vegetables
Fresh and Flavorful**

The water content in
moist vegetables gives
them their characteristic
flavor and texture. It is
important that this
moisture be retained
during the process of
cooking them in the
microwave oven.

To prevent dehydration,
be sure to cover
vegetables with plastic
wrap, leaving a small gap
to allow steam to be
released while they are
cooking.

Onions with Tomatoes and Cream

Level of Difficulty	🍴🔪
Preparation Time	20 min
Cost per Serving	$
Number of Servings	6
Nutritional Value	134 calories 4.5 g protein 4.4 g lipids
Food Exchanges	1/4 oz meat 3 vegetable exchanges 1 fat exchange
Cooking Time	13 min
Standing Time	3 min
Power Level	100%
Write Your Cooking Time Here	

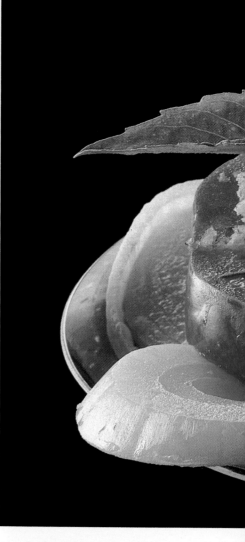

Ingredients
675 g (1-1/2 lb) yellow onions
50 mL (1/4 cup) 18% cream
salt and pepper to taste
675 g (1-1/2 lb) tomatoes
125 mL (1/2 cup) Gruyère cheese, grated
50 mL (1/4 cup) breadcrumbs

Method
— Cut the onions into uniform slices.
— Pour the cream into a dish and add the onions; cover and cook at 100% for 4 minutes, stirring once during the cooking time.
— Season with salt and pepper.
— Slice the tomatoes and layer over the onions.
— Combine the Gruyère and the breadcrumbs and sprinkle over the vegetables.
— Cook at 100% for 8 to 9 minutes, giving the dish a half-turn halfway through the cooking time.
— Let stand for 3 minutes before serving.

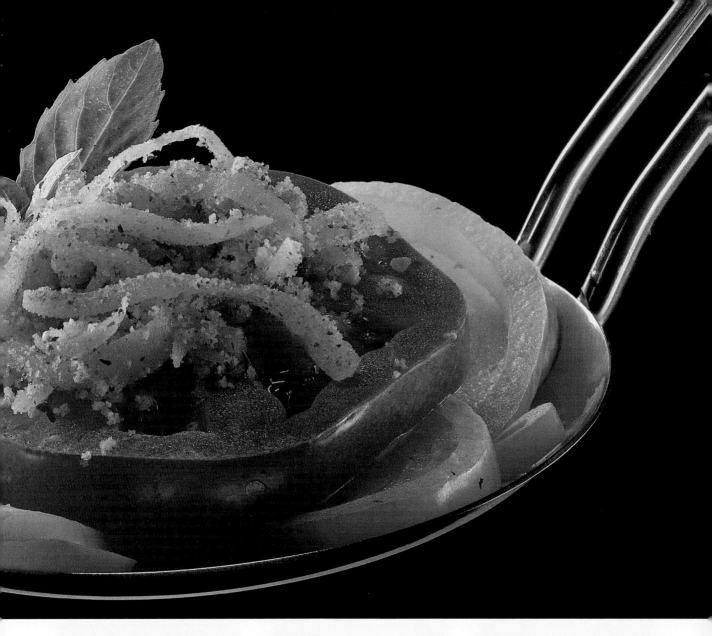

These are the ingredients that should be assembled to prepare this recipe for an original way to serve onions.

Cook the onions in the cream in a covered dish at 100% for 4 minutes.

Layer the tomatoes on top and sprinkle with the mixture of Gruyère and breadcrumbs before the final stage of cooking.

Leeks on a Bed of Noodles

Level of Difficulty	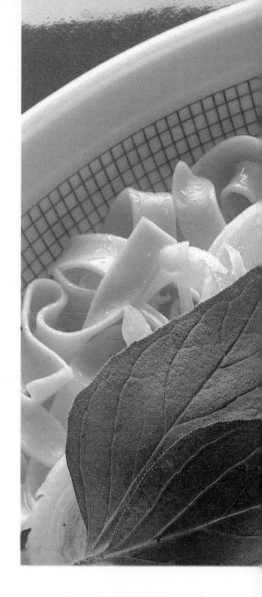
Preparation Time	15 min
Cost per Serving	$
Number of Servings	8
Nutritional Value	192 calories 6 g protein 20.7 g carbohydrate
Food Exchanges	1 oz meat 2 vegetable exchanges 1 bread exchange 1 fat exchange
Cooking Time	20 min
Standing Time	None
Power Level	100%
Write Your Cooking Time Here	

Ingredients
4 leeks, white parts only
500 mL (2 cups) egg noodles
1 L (4 cups) boiling water
5 mL (1 teaspoon) salt
5 mL (1 teaspoon) oil
50 mL (1/4 cup) butter
50 mL (1/4 cup) Gruyère cheese, grated
50 mL (1/4 cup) mozzarella cheese, grated
salt, pepper and paprika to taste

Method
— Add the salt, oil and noodles to the boiling water; cook at 100% for 6 to 8 minutes, stirring twice during the cooking time.
— Drain the noodles, rinse under cold water and set aside.
— Cut the leeks into thin slices, put in a dish and add the butter; cover and cook at 100% for 7 to 9 minutes, stirring once during the cooking time.
— Arrange the noodles in a serving dish and add the leeks.
— Season to taste and sprinkle with the cheeses and the paprika.
— Heat through at 100% for 3 minutes.

MICROTIPS

Avoid Overcooking

Certain foods continue to cook even at the end of the microwave cooking time. For this reason, a **standing time** is usually included in the cooking cycle. A potato may appear to be slightly firm when it comes out of the oven but the heat continues to disperse itself uniformly inside the vegetable while it is standing. It is therefore important to adhere to the **standing times** indicated in microwave recipes. This time will vary according to the food. Remember that the **standing time** is the final step in any recipe and has as much significance as all the steps prior to it.

Gnocchi with Cheese and Tomato Sauce

Level of Difficulty	🍴
Preparation Time	30 min
Cost per Serving	$
Number of Servings	8
Nutritional Value	349 calories 10.1 g protein 27.8 g carbohydrate
Food Exchanges	1 oz meat 1-1/2 bread exchanges 3 fat exchanges
Cooking Time	20 min (+ time for cooking the dumplings in shifts)
Standing Time	None
Power Level	100%, 70%
Write Your Cooking Time Here	

Ingredients
Gnocchi:
900 g (2 lb) potatoes, peeled and cut into 2.5 cm (1 inch) cubes
875 mL (3-1/2 cups) water
45 mL (3 tablespoons) butter
2 eggs
2 egg yolks
250 mL (1 cup) flour
pinch nutmeg
salt and pepper to taste

Cheese and Tomato Sauce:
15 mL (1 tablespoon) butter
2 green onions, chopped
125 mL (1/2 cup) Italian-style tomatoes, chopped
10 mL (2 teaspoons) fine herbs
2 mL (1/2 teaspoon) oregano
2 mL (1/2 teaspoon) basil
250 mL (1 cup) 35% cream
125 mL (1/2 cup) Parmesan cheese, grated
75 mL (1/3 cup) Gruyère cheese, grated

Method
— To prepare the gnocchi, put the potato cubes into a dish and add 125 mL (1/2 cup) of the water; cover and cook at 100% for 6 to 8 minutes, stirring twice during the cooking time.
— Remove the potatoes and set the cooking liquid aside.
— Purée the potatoes and add the butter, eggs, egg yolks, flour, nutmeg, salt and pepper; mix well and set aside.
— Bring the liquid in which the potatoes were cooked plus the remaining 750 mL (3 cups) of water to a boil.
— Using a spoon, drop small amounts of the gnocchi batter into the boiling water.
— Remove the gnocchi as they come to the surface and cool under cold running water.
— Continue until all the batter is used and set the cooked gnocchi aside.

— To prepare the sauce, put the butter into a dish and heat at 100% for 30 seconds.
— Add the green onions and cook at 100% for 2 minutes; add the tomatoes and seasonings and cook at 100% for 2 minutes.
— Add the cream and mix well; reduce the power to 70% and heat through for 2 to 3 minutes, stirring once during the cooking time.
— Add the grated cheeses to thicken the sauce.
— Add the gnocchi and heat at 70% for 3 to 5 minutes, or until well heated through.

MICROTIPS

Higher is Better!

Many recipes instruct you to place the dish on a raised rack in the microwave oven. This technique ensures that the cooking is uniform since the microwaves will also be absorbed from the bottom of the dish. Many different models are available if your oven is not already equipped with a rack.

Salads and Other Cold Appetizers

Salads are sometimes served between the main course and the dessert. They may also be served prior to the main course, following an appetizer. The rules of cuisine should be adapted to each person's taste and rhythm and it is therefore also perfectly acceptable to serve a salad as the appetizer itself.

Sometimes the term salad is used in a way that actually refers to lettuce. This misnomer is quite understandable because so many green salads, which are widely consumed in this country, are made with lettuce as their base. But salads do not have to be made with garden greens only.

The term salad can apply to any combination of cooked and/or uncooked vegetables that are served cold with a dressing or sauce to bring out the flavor. Many cold foods can be used in salads; it is necessary, however, to make sure that all the ingredients used are fresh and crisp. The salad combinations that are possible are infinite and the number of dressings and sauces that can be made to accompany them offers a gread deal of choice.

Various grains, including rice, wheat (cracked or semolina) and corn, may also be used as salad ingredients. These foods contain carbohydrates, protein and Vitamin B. Mixed salads provide balanced dishes which are light and refreshing. Legumes (lentils, chick peas and so on), rich in protein, can be used in salads or puréed to make excellent cold appetizers.

Those who like to work with delicatessen products will enjoy experimenting with Chicken Liver and Pork Pâté (page 94). This pâté, served with small pieces of bread and tiny crackers, is perfect for the cocktail hour, as are the Headcheese (page 96) and the Ham Mousse (page 92).

Well-seasoned marinades bring out the flavor of meats and vegetables, and lighter marinades enhance the flavor of fish. If you are skeptical about the advantages of marinating, the recipe for Marinated Leeks (page 100) should be convincing.

And since seafood is always popular as an appetizer, we have combined it with a choice vegetable in the recipe for Avocados with Seafood (page 98), which is certain to win the approval of all your guests.

Mediterranean Medley

Level of Difficulty	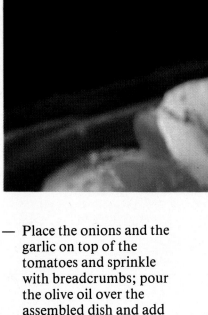
Preparation Time	20 min*
Cost per Serving	**$**
Number of Servings	8
Nutritional Value	120 calories 12 g carbohydrate 7.1 g lipids
Food Exchanges	2 vegetable exchanges 1/4 bread exchange 1-1/2 fat exchanges
Cooking Time	9 min
Standing Time	2 min
Power Level	70%
Write Your Cooking Time Here	

* Leave the eggplant slices to sweat for 30 minutes before cooking them.

Ingredients
450 g (1 lb) eggplant
450 g (1 lb) zucchini
450 g (1 lb) tomatoes
coarse salt
1 onion, finely sliced
1 clove garlic, chopped
75 mL (1/3 cup) Italian
breadcrumbs
50 mL (1/4 cup) olive oil
pepper to taste

Method
— Cut the eggplant into thin slices and sprinkle with coarse salt.
— Leave to sweat for 30 minutes and then rinse well with cold water; drain and pat dry.
— Cut the zucchini into thin slices and cut the tomatoes into cubes.
— Arrange the eggplant in the bottom of a baking dish and layer the zucchini and the tomatoes on top.
— Place the onions and the garlic on top of the tomatoes and sprinkle with breadcrumbs; pour the olive oil over the assembled dish and add pepper to taste.
— Cook at 70% for 7 to 9 minutes, giving the dish a half-turn halfway through the cooking time.
— Let stand for 2 minutes before serving.

This Mediterranean dish is exquisite and suitable for any occasion. First assemble these ingredients.

Sprinkle the eggplant with coarse salt and leave to sweat for 30 minutes.

Layer the vegetables in a baking dish and cook as directed.

Vegetables Oriental Style

Level of Difficulty	
Preparation Time	20 min
Cost per Serving	$
Number of Servings	4
Nutritional Value	169 calories 7.8 g carbohydrate 1 mg iron
Food Exchanges	2 vegetable exchanges 3 fat exchanges
Cooking Time	10 min
Standing Time	5 min
Power Level	100%
Write Your Cooking Time Here	

Ingredients
250 mL (1 cup) broccoli flowerets
250 mL (1 cup) cauliflower flowerets
1 green pepper, cut into strips
1 red pepper, cut into strips
115 g (4 oz) mushrooms, sliced
125 mL (1/2 cup) celery, cut on the bias
50 mL (1/4 cup) oil
15 mL (1 tablespoon) cornstarch
45 mL (3 tablespoons) cold water
250 mL (1 cup) chicken broth
2 mL (1/2 teaspoon) fresh ginger, chopped
pepper to taste

Method
— Preheat a browning dish at 100% for 7 minutes and add the oil; heat at 100% for 30 seconds.
— Sear all the vegetables; cover and cook at 100% for 3 to 5 minutes.
— Let stand for 5 minutes.
— Dissolve the cornstarch in the cold water.
— Heat the chicken broth at 100% for 3 minutes and add the dissolved cornstarch and the ginger, mixing well.
— Cook at 100% for 1 to 2 minutes, stirring halfway through the cooking time and once again at the end.
— Pour the sauce over the vegetables and add pepper to taste before serving.

This recipe, so rich in vegetables, is easy to prepare and is always well received. These are the ingredients required to make this dish.

Cutting the peppers in strips and the celery on the bias will bring out all their flavor in this oriental-style dish.

Pour the sauce over the cooked vegetables and add pepper before serving.

Ham Mousse

Level of Difficulty	🍴🍴
Preparation Time	20 min*
Cost per Serving	$
Number of Servings	6
Nutritional Value	307 calories 17.4 g protein 22.8 g lipids
Food Exchanges	2 oz meat 3-1/2 fat exchanges
Cooking Time	7 min
Standing Time	None
Power Level	100%
Write Your Cooking Time Here	

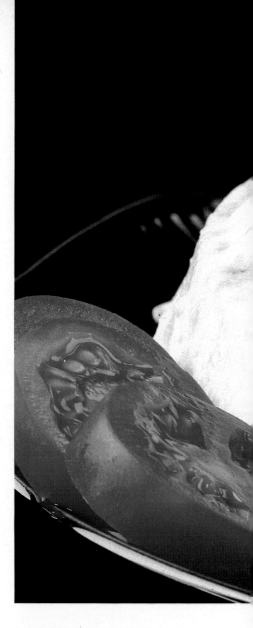

* Refrigerate the ham mousse for 3 hours before serving.

Ingredients
340 g (12 oz) ham, finely chopped
30 mL (2 tablespoons) butter
30 mL (2 tablespoons) flour
375 mL (1-1/2 cups) milk
50 mL (1/4 cup) onion, grated
30 mL (2 tablespoons) Madeira wine
salt and pepper to taste
1 package gelatin
125 mL (1/2 cup) water
250 mL (1 cup) 35% cream

Method
— In a dish, melt the butter at 100% for 40 seconds, add the flour and mix well.
— Pour in the milk and beat vigorously with a whisk; cook at 100% for 4 to 6 minutes, beating twice during the cooking time.
— Add the onion, ham and the Madeira; season to taste and allow to cool.
— Sprinkle the gelatin over the water and set aside for 3 to 4 minutes; heat at 100% for 1 minute, stir well and add to the prepared ham and béchamel.
— Whip the cream until it forms stiff peaks and carefully fold it into the mixture.
— Pour into a mold or into ramekins and refrigerate for about 3 hours before serving.

Beat the béchamel sauce twice with a whisk during the cooking time.

Sprinkle the contents of a package of gelatin over a bowl containing 125 mL (1/2 cup) of water.

Whip the cream and fold it carefully into the ham mixture.

Chicken Liver and Pork Pâté

Level of Difficulty	 (utensils icon)
Preparation Time	25 min*
Cost per Serving	**$**
Number of Servings	24
Nutritional Value	145 calories 8.2 g protein 3.2 g lipids
Food Exchanges	1 oz meat 1-1/2 fat exchanges
Cooking Time	34 min
Standing Time	None
Power Level	90%, 100%, 70%
Write Your Cooking Time Here	(apple/pencil icon)

* The chicken livers must be marinated in the calvados for 5 hours before cooking.

Ingredients

900 g (2 lb) chicken livers
225 g (8 oz) ground pork
125 mL (1/2 cup) calvados
30 mL (2 tablespoons) butter
115 g (4 oz) pork fat
8 green onions, chopped
15 mL (1 tablespoon) parsley, chopped
1 egg, beaten
45 mL (3 tablespoons) 35% cream
50 mL (1/4 cup) Madeira wine
salt and pepper to taste

Method

— Cut the chicken livers in two and marinate them in the calvados for 5 hours in the refrigerator.
— Drain the livers and set the liquid aside.
— Place half the livers in a dish and add the butter; cover and cook at 90% for 5 to 7 minutes, stirring once during the cooking time; allow to cool.
— Combine the cooked and uncooked chicken livers; add the pork fat and chop the mixture. Set aside.
— In a bowl, combine the ground pork, green onions and parsley; add the liver mixture and set aside.
— Combine the egg, cream, Madeira and calvados from the marinade in another bowl; season and mix well.
— Pour the liquid over the meat mixture and mix well.
— Put the mixture into a loaf pan, pressing it down.
— Cook at 100% for 5 minutes; reduce the power to 70% and continue to cook for 18 to 22 minutes, giving the dish a half-turn halfway through the cooking time and draining the fat off four times

during the cooking cycle.
— The terrine is cooked when
  a light incision with a
  knife releases clear liquid.
— Allow to cool and serve on
  crackers or melba toast.

MICROTIPS

Fresh Homegrown Herbs

Herbs have an incomparable flavor, especially when very fresh. A number of herbs can be cultivated in flower pots, like house plants. Dill, basil, chives, coriander, marjoram, parsley, rosemary, savory, sage and thyme all need sunlight. Bay leaves and verbena, on the other hand, grow best in the shade. Chervil, lemon balm, tarragon and mint adapt to either sunlight or shade.

Headcheese

Level of Difficulty	⅋⅋ ⅋⅋
Preparation Time	1 h*
Cost per Serving	$
Number of Servings	18
Nutritional Value	70.3 calories 7.6 g protein
Food Exchanges	1 oz meat
Cooking Time	1 h 45 min
Standing Time	None
Power Level	100%
Write Your Cooking Time Here	

* Refrigerate the headcheese for about 3 hours before serving.

Ingredients
6 pork trotters, split in two
6 cloves
15 mL (1 tablespoon) cinnamon
15 mL (1 tablespoon) salt
2 onions, chopped
1 carrot, grated
2 L (8 cups) water

Method
— Wrap the pork trotters in a cheesecloth and place in a baking dish.
— Add all the other ingredients.
— Cover and cook at 100% for 1 to 1-1/2 hours.
— Remove the trotters and remove the meat from the bones.
— Chop the meat coarsely and return it to the hot cooking liquid.
— Bring to a boil by cooking at 100% for 10 to 15 minutes; remove the fat.
— Pour into a mold or into ramekins and refrigerate for about 3 hours before serving.

Note: For a meatier headcheese use a combination of trotters and hocks.

MICROTIPS

Opening Jars Easily

Is there any experience more frustrating than attempting in vain the simple operation of opening a jar? We have all experienced this frustration to some degree or other. We have two tips to offer you.

Technique No. 1:
The Rubber Band
The difficulty we have in opening jars is usually due to the fact that we are unable to exert sufficient pressure by hand. We can improve our grip by placing a large rubber band around the lid of the jar. If the lid still doesn't open, try placing the jar under hot running water and tapping it with the handle of a knife, without removing the rubber band. Never make dents in the lid!

Technique No. 2:
Perforation
Vacuum-packed jars not previously opened will be easy to open if you make a small perforation in the lid. Simply re-seal the perforation you have made with some tape.

Avocados with Seafood

Ingredients

3 avocados
115 g (4 oz) lobster meat,
cooked and cut into cubes
115 g (4 oz) shrimps, shelled
6 shrimps, unshelled
4 prawn tails
15 mL (1 tablespoon) lemon
juice
50 mL (1/4 cup) mayonnaise
7 mL (1/2 tablespoon)
ketchup
45 mL (3 tablespoons) 35%
cream
15 mL (1 tablespoon) dry
sherry
salt and pepper to taste
2 hard-boiled eggs, chopped

Method

— Cut the avocados in two
  lengthwise and remove the
  seed.
— Using a spoon to remove
  the pulp, leave a 0.5 cm
  (1/4 inch) thick layer
  lining the skin. Dice the
  pulp that has been
  removed.
— Brush the inside of the
  avocados and the diced
  pulp with lemon juice to
  prevent the pulp from
  discoloring and set aside.
— Place the shrimps, shelled
  and unshelled, and the
  prawn tails in a dish;
  cover and cook at 70%
  for 2 to 3 minutes.
— Cut the shelled shrimps
  and the prawn tails into
  cubes; set the unshelled
  shrimps aside for garnish.
— In a bowl, combine the
  mayonnaise, ketchup,
  cream and sherry; mix
  well and season to taste.
— Combine the sauce with
  the seafood and add the
  lobster meat and diced
  avocado pulp.
— Fill the avocados with the
  mixture and sprinkle with
  the chopped eggs.
— Garnish each serving with
  an unshelled shrimp and
  refrigerate before serving.

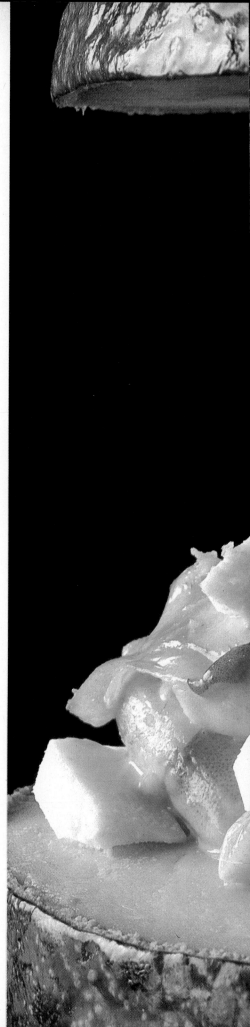

Marinated Leeks

Ingredients
10 leeks
2 celery stalks
75 mL (1/3 cup) olive oil
125 mL (1/2 cup) white wine vinegar

125 mL (1/2 cup) white wine
30 mL (2 tablespoons) fresh parsley, chopped
2 bay leaves
10 peppercorns

Level of Difficulty	🍴🍴
Preparation Time	15 min*
Cost per Serving	**$**
Number of Servings	8
Nutritional Value	112 calories 6 g carbohydrate 9.3 g lipids
Food Exchanges	2 vegetable exchanges 1-1/2 fat exchanges
Cooking Time	10 min
Standing Time	None
Power Level	100%
Write Your Cooking Time Here	✏️🍎

Method
— Remove the green ends from the leeks and set aside for another use.
— Slice the white ends of the leeks lengthwise into strips and cut the celery into julienne strips as well.
— Put in a dish and add all the other ingredients.
— Cover and cook at 100% for 8 to 10 minutes, stirring halfway through the cooking time.
— Let cool before placing in the refrigerator for 12 hours; serve as a salad prior to the meal or with the main course.

* The marinated leeks should be refrigerated for 12 hours before serving.

Mushrooms Greek Style

Ingredients

340 g (12 oz) small, firm mushrooms
45 mL (3 tablespoons) oil
30 mL (2 tablespoons) vinegar

30 mL (2 tablespoons) water
15 mL (1 tablespoon) lemon juice
2 slices lemon
1 bay leaf

pinch thyme
45 mL (3 tablespoons) parsley, chopped
6 peppercorns
salt to taste

Level of Difficulty	🍴
Preparation Time	10 min*
Cost per Serving	$
Number of Servings	6
Nutritional Value	73 calories 7 g lipids
Food Exchanges	1 vegetable exchange 1 fat exchange
Cooking Time	5 min
Standing Time	None
Power Level	100%
Write Your Cooking Time Here	🍎✏️

Method

— Clean the mushrooms with a vegetable brush, pat dry with paper towel and set aside.
— Pour the oil into a baking dish, add all the other ingredients except the mushrooms and heat at 100% for 1 minute.
— Add the mushrooms and cook at 100% for 3 to 4 minutes, stirring once during the cooking time.
— Remove the bay leaf, let cool before placing in the refrigerator for 4 hours and serve very cold.

* The mushrooms should be refrigerated for 4 hours before serving.

Potatoes Stuffed with Sour Cream and Cheese

Ingredients
4 large potatoes, washed but not peeled
30 mL (2 tablespoons) butter, melted
1 egg yolk
50 mL (1/4 cup) sour cream
50 mL (1/4 cup) orange cheddar cheese, grated

Method
— Pierce each potato skin in several places with a fork.
— Put the potatoes in a dish and cook at 100% for 7 to 9 minutes, giving the dish a half-turn halfway through the cooking time.
— Cut a thin slice off the top of each potato.
— Hollow out the potatoes, leaving a 0.5 cm (1/4 inch) layer lining the skin on the inside.
— In a bowl, combine the potato pulp with the butter, egg yolk and sour cream and mix well.
— Stuff the potatoes with the mixture and sprinkle with the cheddar cheese.
— Cook at 100% for 3 to 5 minutes, giving the dish a half-turn halfway through the cooking time.
— Let stand for 2 minutes.

Potatoes with a Garlic Stuffing

Ingredients
6 potatoes
30 mL (2 tablespoons) flour
250 mL (1 cup) milk
45 mL (3 tablespoons) 35%
cream
45 mL (3 tablespoons)
parsley, chopped
salt and pepper to taste
12 cloves garlic, chopped
125 mL (1/2 cup) butter
paprika to garnish

Method
— Pierce the skin of each
  potato in several places
  with a fork.
— Put the potatoes in a dish
  and cook at 100% for 10
  to 12 minutes, giving the
  dish a half-turn after 6
  minutes of cooking.
— Cut a thin slice off the top
  of each potato.
— Hollow out the potatoes,
  leaving a 0.5 cm (1/4 inch)
  layer lining the skin
  inside.
— In a bowl, combine the
  potato pulp with the
  flour, milk, cream,
  parsley, salt and pepper;
  mix well and set aside.
— Put the garlic in a dish and
  add the butter; cook at
  100% for 3 minutes,
  stirring once during the
  cooking time.
— Combine the butter and
  garlic with the pulp
  mixture and stuff the
  potatoes with the resulting
  filling.
— Sprinkle with paprika.
— Cook at 100% for 5 to 6
  minutes, giving the dish a
  half-turn halfway through
  the cooking time.
— Let stand for 2 minutes.

Some Suggestions for Harmony

Here are some suggestions for combinations of appetizers and main dishes, many taken from this and other volumes in our *Microwave Magic* series, that we feel would balance each other quite nicely. So many different variations and combinations are possible that the best rules to follow are probably your own experience and imagination.

Bon appétit!

Two Menus for All Seasons

Zucchini Stuffed with Veal
Fish Amandine (with a lemon and almond sauce)
or
Veal Marsala (with a wine sauce)
Eggplant and Tomato Fricassee
Lamb Cutlets Harissa (with a hot sauce)
or
Roast Leg of Lamb with Herbs

Summer Dinner Menu

Avocados with Seafood
Beef Heart Kebabs
or
Grilled Tournedos with Wine Sauce

Small Cold Buffet for Two

Chicken Liver and Pork Pâté
Herbed Bread
Red Cabbage and Nut Salad

Menus with Marinades

Marinated Leeks
or
Marinated Flank Steak
or
Seviche (marinated raw fish)

Summer Buffet

Mini Poultry Kebabs
Cauliflower Quiche
Shrimp Salad
Green Salad with Roquefort
Tomato and Avocado Salad

Glossary

Aromatic: A plant, leaf or herb with a strong and penetrating aroma, used to give a special flavor to foods. Examples include saffron, chervil, tarragon, bay leaves and thyme.

Aspic: A cold dish made with diced, cooked or uncooked foods, molded in a jelly—usually a stock set with gelatin. Aspics are very decorative and are an attractive addition to any table.

Baste: To coat the surface of meat or pastry with melted butter, oil, other liquid ingredients or beaten eggs, with the aid of a pastry brush.

Binding agent: Foods, usually with a large quantity of starch, that are added to stuffings to give them the necessary body and texture to hold together. Breadcrumbs, cooked rice and potatoes are common binding agents; cream and beaten eggs are sometimes used as well.

Filling/Stuffing: A mixture of raw or cooked ingredients, finely or coarsely chopped or puréed and used to fill the cavities of meat or vegetables.

Hollow out: To remove the flesh, or edible substance, from any food (vegetables, crustaceans, eggs, fish and so on), without breaking the outside skin or shell, for the purpose of filling it.

Marinate: To place meat, poultry, fish or vegetables in a mixture of oil and lemon juice, wine or vinegar with seasonings, usually for several hours, to tenderize and flavor the food.

Mayonnaise: An uncooked emulsion of egg yolks, oil and lemon juice, mayonnaise is a thick and smooth cold sauce served with cold dishes and salads. A number of other cold sauces are variations on mayonnaise.

Mousse:	A cold preparation composed of a combination of gelatin and other ingredients which are puréed, such as chicken, fish or vegetables. It is light in texture and appropriate as an appetizer.
Offal:	The edible parts, other than its meat, of any animal. The heart, liver, tongue and kidneys are considered offal.
Season:	To add spices, herbs, aromatics, salt or pepper to dishes to enhance their flavor.
Sheet of dough:	Raw pastry that is rolled out with a rolling pin and used to make tarts, crusts for pâtés, turnovers and so on. When cooked, the pastry becomes the crust.
Slice:	To cut vegetables, fruits or meats into very thin slices.
Smoking:	A method of preserving that consists of placing foods, usually meat or fish, on suspended grills over a fire using certain types of wood for flavor. Aromatic seasonings are also put into the fire, their flavor penetrating the food being smoked as well.
Thickening agent:	Any mixture used to thicken bouillons or sauces that are too thin. Common thickeners include roux (cooked butter and flour), kneaded butter (a mixture of uncooked butter and flour), and a combination of beaten egg yolks and cream. Flour, cornstarch and arrowroot, dissolved in cold water, are also used to thicken sauces.
Vinaigrette:	A cold, clear sauce or salad dressing made with oil, vinegar or lemon juice, spices, salt and pepper and served with cold dishes and salads.

Culinary Terms

Have you ever been given a menu and found that you were unable to understand many of the words? There are many different culinary terms, some of which are rather obscure. Here is a short glossary of some that may help you.

A la diable: A piquant sauce based on vinegar, wine or lemon juice, with mustard and cayenne.

A la grecque: An oil-based dressing, sauce or marinade with lemon juice as a main ingredient. Tomatoes and black olives may also be added.

Aioli: Mayonnaise sauce heavily laced with garlic.

Au Roquefort: A salad dressing made with Roquefort cheese.

Harissa: A North African sauce made with a purée of small pimentos mixed with oil, garlic, coriander and cayenne.

Marinière: A combination of white wine and seasoning in which fish and seafood, especially mussels, are cooked and served.

Provençale: A sauce or garnish with tomatoes and garlic as main ingredients.

Seviche: Raw fish marinated in lemon or lime juice and seasonings.

Taboulé: A Lebanese dish, based on cracked wheat with finely chopped tomatoes, mint and fresh parsley.

Conversion Chart

Conversion Chart for the Main Measures Used in Cooking

Volume
1 teaspoon	5 mL
1 tablespoon	15 mL
1 quart (4 cups)	1 litre
1 pint (2 cups)	500 mL
1/2 cup	125 mL
1/4 cup	50 mL

Weight
2.2 lb	1 kg (1000 g)
1.1 lb	500 g
0.5 lb	225 g
0.25 lb	115 g
1 oz	30 g

Metric Equivalents for Cooking Temperatures

49°C	120°F	120°C	250°F
54°C	130°F	135°C	275°F
60°C	140°F	150°C	300°F
66°C	150°F	160°C	325°F
71°C	160°F	180°C	350°F
77°C	170°F	190°C	375°F
82°C	180°F	200°C	400°F
93°C	200°F	220°C	425°F
107°C	225°F	230°C	450°F

Readers will note that, in the recipes, we give 250 mL as the equivalent for 1 cup and 450 g as the equivalent for 1 lb and that fractions of these measurements are even less mathematically accurate. The reason for this is that mathematically accurate conversions are just not practical in cooking. Your kitchen scales are simply not accurate enough to weigh 454 g—the true equivalent of 1 lb—and it would be a waste of time to try. The conversions given in this series, therefore, necessarily represent approximate equivalents, but they will still give excellent results in the kitchen. No problems should be encountered if you adhere to either metric or imperial measurements throughout a recipe.

Index

MICROTIPS